LIFE ISSUES

TEENAGE PREGNANCY

by Gisela Meier

Marshall Cavendish
NEW YORK • LONDON • TORONTO • SYDNEY

Published by Marshall Cavendish Corporation
2415 Jerusalem Avenue
North Bellmore, New York 11710
USA

Library of Congress Cataloging-in-Publication Data

Meier, Gisela.
    Teenage pregnancy / by Gisela Meier.
      p.   cm. — (Life Issues)
    Includes bibliographical references and index.
    Summary: Gives the young reader important facts about being
sexually active, becoming pregnant, and having and raising a baby,
as well as alternatives such as abortion or adoption.
    ISBN 1-85435-611-9
    1. Teenage mothers—United STates—Juvenile literature.
    2. Teenage pregnancy—United States—Juvenile literature.
    3. Teenage parents—United States—Juvenile literature.
    [1. Teenage mothers. 2. Pregnancy. 3. Teenage parents.]
    I. Title. II. Series.
    HQ759.4.M45 1993
    306.7′0835—dc20   93-14169
                                           CIP
                                           AC

Produced by The Creative Spark
Editor: Gregory Lee
Art direction: Robert Court
Design: Mary Francis-DeMarois, Robert Court
Page layout, graphic illustration: Mary Francis-DeMarois

Marshall Cavendish Editorial Director: Evelyn M. Fazio
Marshall Cavendish Editorial Consultant: Marylee Knowlton

Printed and bound in the United States of America

Photographic Note
Several persons depicted in this book are photographic models; their appearance in these photographs is solely to
dramatize some of the situations and choices facing readers of the Life Issues series.

Photo Credits
Christie Costanzo p. 4,6,11, 13, 14, 18, 20, 25, 26, 32, 43, 44, 47, 54, 56, 60, 62, 64, 66, 68, 72, 76, 80, 84, 87
Wide World Photos p. 36, 50, 52
Posters on pages 17, 29, and 38 reprinted by permission of the Children's Defense Fund.

Cover photo: PhotoEdit (Jose Carillo)

Acknowledgements
The author wishes to thank all of the individuals, particularly the teenagers, who were interviewed for this book.
Their names have been changed to protect their privacy.
Editorial Consultant: Julie Frauenfelder, Coordinator, Yonkers Adolescent Pregnancy Prevention and Services Program

TABLE OF CONTENTS

PROLOGUE

Stephanie's face gets hot and tears fill her eyes as she looks at the dipstick from the home pregnancy test. It has turned blue. That means she is pregnant.

It can't be, she thinks. This can't be happening to me. What am I going to do? I'm only 16!

A hundred questions seem to fill her mind all at once. What will my boyfriend say? Will he stick by me or dump me? Should I get an abortion? Can I keep the baby? What will everyone at school think of me? How can I ever tell mom and dad?

Sitting locked in her bathroom, Stephanie feels like she is all alone. But all across the country, on this same day, more than 3,000 other teenage girls have discovered that they are pregnant. Like Stephanie, most of them feel panic and confusion over something they didn't think would happen. Most of them are unmarried. Some are as young as 11 years old.

Every year, more than one million teenage girls in America become pregnant. Each of them must make tough decisions that will have serious consequences for them, their families, and the babies they may have. For all of these girls, life will never be the same again.

What happens to them also creates enormous costs for the United States government and taxpayers. Teenagers who become parents usually have a very difficult time becoming independent, self-supporting adults. Many of them rely on financial support from their families or the government for many years.

Because of the way it affects individual lives and our country as a whole, teenage pregnancy is one of the biggest problems facing the United States today.

1

PRESSURES AND CHOICES

"Sex oozes from every pore of the culture and there's not a kid in the world who can avoid it."
—Charles Krauthammer

It's tough being a teenager. For young people between the ages of 12 and 20, everything seems to be changing. Their bodies are being transformed from a child to an adult. Their daily routines are no longer simply defined, and their feelings about themselves and other people are quite different than before.

Teenagers are no longer children, but they are not yet adults. As they try to decide what kind of adults they want to be, they begin making choices that will affect them for the rest of their lives.

Teenagers go through a lot of changes. The most obvious changes are physical. Sometime between the ages of 10 and 14, young people suddenly become taller and their bodies change in dramatic ways. A girl develops breasts and a more womanly figure. Her ovaries start to release eggs, and she begins to menstruate. A boy's body becomes more muscular. His voice deepens, and he grows more hair on his face and body. His genitals become larger and begin to produce sperm.

For many teenagers, these physical changes cause a lot of stress and unhappiness. For one thing, they don't happen at the same age for everyone. Teens who develop earlier than their friends often feel self-conscious and embarrassed. Those who are slower to develop may feel inferior and wait anxiously for signs that they too are growing up.

Teenagers must cope with many different kinds of stress, including making new friends and forming romantic relationships.

Some teens feel awkward and clumsy for a period of time as their bodies grow and develop. They worry a great deal about how they look and what other people think of them. They fret about their figures, their complexions, their hair, and their clothes.

Since they are no longer children, teenagers become more independent of their parents. They spend more time away from home and make more decisions for themselves. This growing sense of independence is an important step to becoming an adult. The new freedom, however, can be both exciting and frightening.

"You want the freedom, you want to do what you want," said 15-year-old Erica. "But it's scary, too, because you're not sure of yourself and you're not sure about what you want to do. You're wondering who you want to be, but to your friends you want to project that you have it all together, that you're cool."

There are big changes in a teenager's social life as well. As they separate themselves from their parents, young people long to be accepted and appreciated by their peers. They want to belong to a group.

"Most teenagers look to what other teens are doing as a guide as far as the clothes they wear and the way they act," said Erica. "They go with the trend. It's very important to dress and act in a way that makes you fit into the group. You have to fit in, otherwise you're not really going to have friends. You try not to show that you're self-conscious, but usually you are. You don't want to look like you're trying to be cool, you just want to look like you *are* cool."

"Nobody wants to be an outcast, especially teenage boys, because that could ruin you," said 19-year-old Mike. "So most kids try to do what the people do, follow the crowd. What other people say is more important than what you think. That's the mentality."

Teenagers also begin thinking about the opposite sex in a very different way. Because of the physical changes they are going through, they begin to have sexual feelings toward each other. They spend more time with members of the opposite sex and start dating. They may experiment with kissing, hugging, and other forms of sexual expression.

PRESSURES REGARDING SEX

Most teenagers think about sex. They are curious about their new feelings and wonder what it would be like to have a sexual relationship. This is a natural part of growing up. Many teenagers also come under a lot of pressure to start having sex. This pressure comes at them from several different directions. Among their classmates at school, for instance, sex is likely to become a major topic of conversation.

"It's a big subject that everyone likes to talk about," said 15-year-old Laurie. "You hear guys talk about it in their little groups, and my friends talk about it, too. There are always questions about sex like, `Are you a virgin?' If you say yes, then they'll try to make a joke out of it, and then they'll tell people."

"There's a lot of pressure at school to do it," said 16-year-old Rhonda. "The guys are pressuring you. Your friends who are sexually active say, `Oh, you're a wimp. It's nothing big, just do it.'"

Boys often find that they are being pushed to prove themselves by "scoring."

"To the guys, sex is like a sport," said Mike. "You've got to make points. If you're not having sex, you're not going to fit in with the crowd."

Teens also notice how much sex there is in the media—the television shows they watch, the movies they see, and the music they listen to. According to one study, there are about 65,000 sexual acts or comments on prime-time television every year. Most of the sex on television and in the movies involves people who are not married. The couples rarely worry about birth control or protecting themselves from sexually transmitted diseases (STDs). They are hardly ever shown suffering any consequences—such as an unwanted pregnancy or an STD—as a result of having sex. In the movies and on TV, sex looks easy, fun, and glamorous. It appears to be something everyone is doing.

"You can't even turn on a commercial without seeing breasts or someone kissing and touching someone," said Rhonda. "Sex is really overrated, and people think it's better than it is. So kids think it's something that has to be done."

On the other hand, teenagers are also being told that sex is something that shouldn't be done. Parents, teachers and religious leaders tell teenagers that sex should be saved for marriage. Young people are caught between two sets of messages: one side says, "Go!" and the other says, "Stop!"

Girls even get conflicting messages from their peers. "If you're a virgin, you're a prude," said Laurie. "And if you're not, then you're just totally the town slut. You just can't be a nice person either way."

All of this pressure can create a lot of confusion for a teenager. He or she may have a lot of questions about sex, but may not know where to go for the answers. Most teens are too embarrassed to talk to their parents about sex, and many schools provide little or no sex education. Teenagers often rely on their friends for information. Unfortunately, that information is not always accurate.

When a young person becomes involved with a boyfriend or girlfriend, the couple may have to deal with pressures directly. For example, one might pressure the other to have sex, using arguments such as:

"Everybody's doing it."
"If you don't have sex with me, I'll break up with you."
"If you love me, prove it."
"Don't you want to find out what it feels like?"
"We've gone this far, it's too late to stop."
"This will prove that you are a man (woman)."

DECIDING ABOUT HAVING SEX

More teenagers than ever before are deciding to have sex, many of them starting at a very young age. A girl is more likely to think of sex as something romantic, an expression of love between her and her boyfriend. Many girls, however, have sex with boys with whom they have no real relationship. Love has nothing to do with it.

"I have a lot of friends who think they have to have sex to get a guy to like them," said Rhonda. "They say they're enjoying it, but they're really not, because they're doing it because they feel they have to."

For many boys, having sex is just a way to prove their manhood. "For a lot of guys, it's a big game," said 19-year-old Jerry. "Like who can get the most girls. It's all guys think about and all they want to do. With my buddies, when they're out, it's like a competition to see who can get the girls and who can do the most in the least amount of time."

Some girls drift into sexual activity without a clear idea of why they are doing so.

"I started having sex when I was 12," said Candy. "Nobody was ever there to stop me. My mom wasn't around. I was always all by myself. I had nobody to teach me right from wrong. I hung around with a lot of older kids, and it's what everybody was doing."

"It just happened," said Ramona. "I was 14, in eighth grade. I don't know, I guess I just wanted to know what it was like or something."

"You don't really say, well, I'm going to have sex this day," said Sandy. "When it happens, it happens. And you're not really thinking because you're young, so you don't think, well, I'm going to get pregnant, or anything like that. It just happens to you."

Sometimes alcohol or drugs play a part in a teenager's decision to have sex. A person who is drinking alcohol or using drugs is less likely to be cautious and responsible about their behavior. Under the influence of these substances, teenagers sometimes take chances they otherwise wouldn't. They may ignore their previous decision not to have sex, or may be careless about using protection against pregnancy and disease.

On the other hand, there are many teens who make a definite choice not to have sex until they are older. Some have decided, because of their religious beliefs or other reasons, that they will wait until they are married. Some realize that having sex could lead to problems that would get in the way of their plans for the future. Others worry about diseases they could catch.

"Sex is not a big topic with the people I hang out with," said Erica. "We want to get good grades in school so we can go to a good college. Guys aren't exactly on the back burner, but it's not what we talk about all the time."

Young males often experience a great deal of peer pressure to have sex.

MYTHS ABOUT SEX

Teenagers often learn about sex from other teenagers. Unfortunately, some of the things they learn are false. The following are just a few examples of myths about sex:

• You can't get pregnant the first time you have sex.

• You can't get pregnant if you have intercourse standing up.

• If you have sex a lot, you won't get pregnant.

• If you don't have sex a lot, you won't get pregnant.

• You can't get pregnant in a hot tub.

• If a girl douches with a soft drink after sex, she won't get pregnant.

• If you jump up and down after intercourse, you won't get pregnant.

• A girl can't get pregnant during her period.

• Taking a birth control pill just before intercourse will prevent pregnancy.

• If you have sex while you are drunk, you can't get pregnant.

All of the above statements are completely false. The facts are these:

• The biological purpose of sex is to reproduce.

• As soon as a girl begins ovulating and a boy begins producing sperm, they are capable of creating a baby.

• Unless there is something physically wrong with one of them, a boy and a girl run the risk of beginning a pregnancy every time they have sexual intercourse.

• One out of every 20 girls becomes pregnant the first time she has sex.

• One in every five becomes pregnant during the first month of sexual activity.

• Couples who have sex 12 times run a fifty percent chance of starting a pregnancy.

Carlos, who is 18, also has decided that sex can wait: "At our school, all the guys brag about the fact that they have a girlfriend, and they only want her for one thing: sex. I very calmly ask them: 'If you are going to do that, what is the point of having a girlfriend that you are supposed to love, because sex is not love.' Their response is: 'Oh, you aren't living in the current ages, you should be more sexually active.' So I tell them, 'Fine, we'll play it your way. And when you come up with a disease that leaves you scratching at night, I want you to remember you're hipper than I am.'"

PREGNANCY

Yolanda was 17 years old when she met Rudy, who was also 17. Up to that time, she hadn't dated very many guys.

"I wasn't really into that," she said. "I was going to school and working. That's where I met my boyfriend, at my job. We started liking each other. We started going places together, and we ended up going to his house. First we'd stay outside, then later we started going in to watch TV. Then we went into his room, and that's when we started having sex. I wanted to wait until I got married, but I didn't.

"I didn't use any kind of birth control because I didn't know anything about sex. I would just hear what people would tell me, but I hadn't experienced it, so I didn't know what it was about.

Many teenage girls merely hope that they aren't pregnant, but sooner or later they will be unable to ignore it. Girls who suspect they are pregnant should have a pregnancy test early because prenatal care is important for the baby's health.

"I would worry about getting pregnant, but after my period would come I would be relieved, and I wouldn't worry about it. But the next month I was there worrying, waiting for my period. I would say to myself, I'm not going to get pregnant, I'm not, I'm not. Then one day my period didn't come. And the next month it didn't come. By the time I went for a pregnancy test, I was already four months pregnant."

Most teenage girls who have sex believe, or hope, that they will not get pregnant. Some of them think they are too young to get pregnant. Others have not learned the facts about contraception.

Some teenagers are aware of contraceptives, but they don't use them. They may find it too awkward and embarrassing to discuss birth control with their partner. Going to a doctor for advice on birth control or buying a contraceptive device in a store is just too scary. Some of the reasons young people give for not using birth control are:

> "I was only 14 years old. I guess I knew what birth control was, but I didn't really care."
>
> "I was too embarrassed to talk to my parents about it."
>
> "I didn't know where to go to get birth control."
>
> "Why should I wear a condom? It's the girl's responsibility to take care of birth control."
>
> "My mom said, `If you need birth control just come and ask me.' But I didn't want her to know what I was doing."
>
> "I don't like the way a condom feels."

Some teenager girls do not want to take birth control pills because they believe the pills cause side effects or serious health problems. Actually, side

Many teenage girls are afraid to ask their parents about ways to prevent pregnancy. If so, they should seek help from a health clinic or counseling service that can give them sound advice.

effects such as nausea, weight gain, and dizziness are usually minor and disappear after a time. Taking the pill rarely causes major medical complications for a healthy woman under the age of 25, especially if she doesn't smoke.

Teenage girls also refuse to take birth control pills because doing so can give them a bad reputation.

"If you use birth control, you're considered to be a little tramp," said Laurie. "It means you can go off and have sex with anybody because of the fact that you are protected. That's just a sign of saying you like sex and you do it all the time. Some girls have to take the pill to regulate their periods, and I don't think guys know that. If they find out a girl is on the pill, I think guys would really tease her. I think rumors would go around the school."

Many teenagers, particularly girls, have romantic ideas about sex. They believe that if they are swept away in a moment of passion and end up having sex, it proves they are in love. Preparing for sex ahead of time by obtaining a contraceptive is something only a "slut" would do. Girls who believe this often end up with a pregnancy—and without a boyfriend.

Teenagers who do use contraceptives may use them incorrectly. The pill, for example, must be taken every day at the same time as prescribed, otherwise it is not effective. If a girl forgets to take it, even once or twice, she can end up pregnant. Condoms also must be used correctly, otherwise they can break or leak. Some boys have picked up the mistaken notion that using two condoms is better than one. Actually, this makes it more likely that both condoms will tear.

Other kinds of birth control methods are not very effective, such as withdrawal, a method where the couple stops having intercourse before the boy ejaculates. This rarely works, however, because enough semen carrying the sperm can escape from the penis well before the boy ejaculates, and cause pregnancy.

Another ineffective method is called rhythm. This means the couple only has sex when the girl is least likely to get pregnant—at least, that's what the couple hopes. This is very difficult to do—especially for a girl whose periods have not yet become regular. Also, many teenagers do not have a clear idea when during a girl's cycle she is least likely to become pregnant.

Not all teenage pregnancies are accidental. Melanie was 14 when she fell in love with a 16-year-old boy. "I wanted to get pregnant because I loved him, and he loved me," she said. "Everything was fine. But then he started getting involved with drugs and his friends because he was still a kid himself. He still wanted to go party."

Teenage girls have a number of reasons for wanting to have a baby. Often they come from families where they have received little affection and attention. They think a baby will give them someone to love and someone who will love them in return. They may also believe that a pregnancy will force their boyfriends to marry them. Some girls get pregnant because they see how much

BIRTH CONTROL

Several different methods of contraception or birth control are available today. Some work better than others, but none works 100 percent of the time. The most common types of birth control are:

- **CONDOM**, or "rubber" — A thin, flexible covering that a male wears over his penis during sex. Effective 88 percent of the time, a condom is more effective if used with foam.
- **DEPO-PROVERA** — The newest form of contraception, this birth control drug is given to a woman by injection about every three months by a doctor. Effective more than 99 percent of the time.
- **DIAPHRAGM** — A small rubber cup that fits over the lower portion and opening of the uterus (cervix) located at the top of the vagina. Effective 82 percent of the time.
- **FOAM** — A chemical put inside the female's vagina before sex. Effective 79 percent of the time, foam is more effective if used with a condom.
- **IUD**, or intrauterine device — A small device put inside the uterus through the cervix by a doctor. Effective 95 percent of the time.
- **NORPLANT** — Tiny capsules of a birth control substance in a rod inserted under the skin of a woman's arm by a physician. This can stay in place for five years, and is effective more than 99 percent of the time.
- **PILL** — A prescription drug that must be taken every day as prescribed in order to work. Effective 97 percent of the time.
- **SPONGE** — A small, soft sponge placed over the cervix like a diaphragm. Effective 72 percent of the time.

The only method of birth control that is effective 100 percent of the time, other than an operation that permanently prevents pregnancy, is abstinence, which means not having sex at all.

attention a pregnant woman receives. They think their own mothers will want to take care of them if they have a baby. Others hope to get back at their parents or prove that they are adults.

Teenage girls most likely to get pregnant on purpose are those not doing well in school, especially if they come from poor families. They may have few goals for their lives and little hope that things will get better. They don't have any reason not to get pregnant.

There are, however, many reasons why teenagers should not get pregnant. For example, it can be a very traumatic experience. Nicole found this out when she became pregnant at the age of 14. She tells her story:

"Mine was an odd pregnancy. I skipped one month, but then I got my period for the rest of the other months. So I didn't think that I was pregnant. When I started getting big and the baby started moving, that's when I thought I was. I had already broken up with my boyfriend, and I was dating someone else. So I didn't bother telling him. I didn't tell my parents because I was too scared. I hid my pregnancy for the whole nine months. Afterwards nobody could believe it, because I'm so skinny. I didn't get very big. No one knew I was pregnant.

"It was scary. I didn't know what to do. I felt so guilty the whole time because I was hiding it. It's like a feeling inside that's so ugly. But I

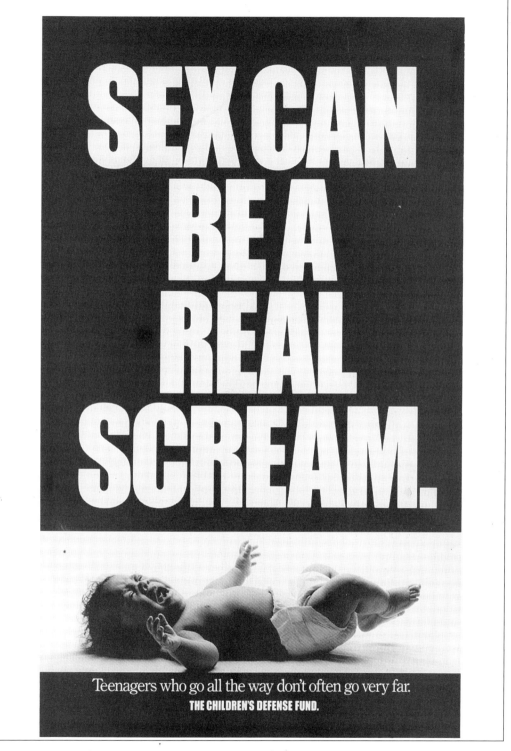

Many teens end up getting pregnant to prove they are adults. Too few think about the consequences of having and raising a baby as a teenager.

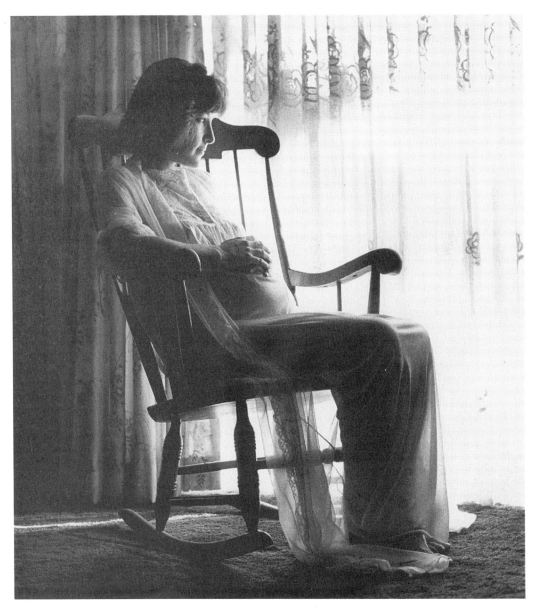

Teenage mothers must often live with other relatives before and after the pregnancy because many times their own parents refuse to let them stay at home.

was more scared of what my parents would do, because my dad is kind of violent. My grandmother kept asking me, 'Are you pregnant?' I would just say no.

"I had the baby at home in the bathroom, all by myself. My brothers were home, but they were in another part of the house. I started at one o'clock in the morning with contractions. I didn't think anything because I get bad cramps, and it wasn't that bad. I thought I was getting my period. I figured, it's not really time yet. Then it was getting harder, and I felt like I had to use the restroom, but it wasn't that.

It was that the baby had to come out. I think I was in shock, so it wasn't as painful as they say. I didn't think about it. I lay on the floor and pushed. She came out real easy.

"Then I wasn't sure what to do about the umbilical cord. I wasn't sure what would happen if I didn't cut it. But I know that they do cut it, so I cut it with my fingernails. She was a strong baby. She didn't cry really loud so they didn't hear her. I washed her and everything, and then I called my older brother. I told him that I had had a baby, and he didn't believe me. So I had to open the door and show him, and then he believed me. He panicked. He didn't know what to do. I told him to call the hospital, but he was too scared.

"I was so scared that I was going to get in so much trouble. I was cleaning the bathroom, and I guess from losing too much blood I would faint. I was just cleaning and cleaning, because I was so terrified that I was going to get in trouble.

"After that, we got a phone call from my grandparents and my brother told them to come over right away, that something was wrong, but he wouldn't tell them what. When they came over, I was lying down and holding my baby. I'm terrified of my grandpa because he used to beat me all the time. I started crying. My grandma asked me, 'What's this?' I told her, 'It's my baby.' She didn't believe me at first, and then she blew up.

"They took me to the hospital and they kept me there overnight because I had lost so much blood. They took my baby away and put her in a children's hospital because she wasn't born in a sterile environment, to make sure she didn't catch anything. They let her go home after two weeks.

"I was so terrified to see my dad. I didn't know what he was going to do. I wanted to be the perfect daughter for him. I was scared of letting him down. I expected him to blow up and yell. But he surprised me. He was very calm. He just said he'd be there for me and we'd deal with it. I really thought he would make me give her up, but he said, 'No, it's your baby, I couldn't do that.'

"I live with my stepmother and my dad. I don't get along with my stepmother. One time I got in a fight with her and she called me a 'slut.' That really hurt me. She's always putting me down and she makes her kids seem better than me. She's not there for me when I need her.

"It's harder talking to my dad because he's the type of person, he interrupts you. He doesn't let you finish what you want to say. So I don't talk to him. But he does try hard, he helps me a lot. He's attached to the baby and I'm worried about that because when I want to move out it's going to be hard for him.

"The baby's father went to the hospital to see the baby. I guess he expected the whole thing to be one big happy family. But I don't want to be with him, so I told him no. He drank too much, he wasn't responsible and he didn't have a job. I didn't want that kind of life for my baby."

Nicole made it through a terrifying pregnancy and birth, but her troubles were just beginning. At the age of 14, she had become a mother. She would have to deal with the consequences for the rest of her life.

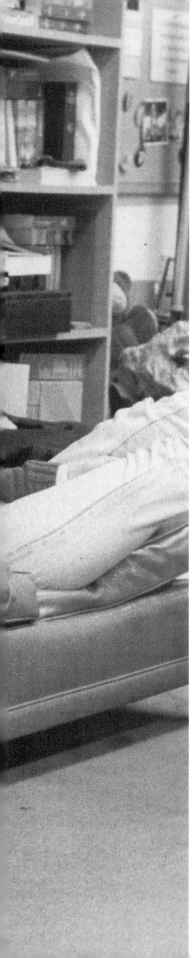

2

THE CONSEQUENCES OF TEENAGE PREGNANCY

"Having sex is not cool. It's not so much fun, because then you've got to pay the consequences. The reality is that you're going to be stuck with a little girl or a little boy, and all you're going to be doing is suffering with your baby."
—Karen, 18-year-old mother

When a teenage girl becomes pregnant, it can change her life forever. She will have to make some of the most serious and important decisions of her life. All of the plans and dreams that she had for herself may have to change. Her pregnancy, and her decisions about it, will also have serious consequences for her baby, the father of her child, her and the boy's parents, and other family members.

Needless to say, the first person who has to deal with a teenage pregnancy is the girl herself. "I was shocked," said Rhonda, who found out she was pregnant when she was 15. "It was like I couldn't believe I was pregnant. I was upset with myself, wondering how my boyfriend was going to feel about it and what people would think of me."

"When I got pregnant I almost wanted to die because I was so scared of my family," said 16-year-old Jessica. "I was really petrified."

Many girls keep their pregnancy secret for several months. They try to pretend, even to

When a teenager first learns she is pregnant, she often will not tell anyone—not even the baby's father—about her predicament.

themselves, that nothing has happened. "I was afraid," said 16-year-old Melanie. "I kept telling myself, I'm not pregnant, I'm not pregnant." It wasn't until her mother noticed her changing body five months later that the secret came out.

No matter how hard she tries to avoid it, sooner or later the pregnant teenager will have to face reality and make some tough choices. First she has to decide whether to have an abortion or have the baby. If she chooses to have the baby, she must decide whether to keep it or give it up for adoption.

How will her boyfriend react? Many boys stay with their girlfriends and do their best to help them through whatever decisions they make. For other boys, the beginning of a pregnancy means the end of a relationship. "I know a lot of my friends who were going out with their boyfriends two or three years," said 16-year-old Rachel. "Then they got pregnant, and all of a sudden it's like, `What's your name again? I'm sorry, I don't think I know you.'"

The teenager will also have to face her family. Some girls manage to get an abortion without ever telling their parents, but most girls have to deal with the dreaded task of telling mom or dad. Typical reactions from parents are shock, anger, sadness, and disappointment. Some parents can't accept the pregnancy and force their daughters to leave home. Others are caring and supportive. Sometimes there are arguments about what should be done. The parents, for instance, may want their daughter to have an abortion, while the girl wants to keep the baby.

A DIFFICULT DECISION

When 18-year-old Yolanda became pregnant, she was caught between the wishes of her mother and her boyfriend, Rudy. She tells how the situation was resolved:

"My mom took me to the clinic and they told me I was pregnant. She was real hurt and real mad. She said not to tell anybody I was pregnant, that we were going to go down and get an abortion. She said she would pay for everything. She said I wasn't ready to be a mother, that I would probably leave the baby to her and she had too many responsibilities and problems. I told Rudy and he said, 'No, we're going to keep this baby.'

"One day, my mom said, 'Tomorrow we're going; I have the money.' Rudy came over that night and we were talking and we were both crying. He said, 'Tonight I'm going to pick you up and we're leaving.' I said, 'We can't go anywhere, we don't have any money.' He said we would go to Chicago, because he had some relatives there.

"Then I said, 'Why don't we just talk to her and tell her how we feel? We'll tell her you'll quit school and go to work. You'll go to night school and I'll stay in school.' We went to my grandma. She's like a mom to me and she was more understanding. She went and talked to my mom and made her understand. Grandma said, 'Maybe God sent the baby to her so she can settle down now and have her family.' She said, 'Just give her a chance.' So my mom said okay. I went into labor on my mom's birthday and I had my baby the next day."

Any decision the girl makes will be difficult. If she decides to have an abortion, she might have to cope with feelings of sorrow and guilt. If she gives the baby up for adoption, she may grieve over the loss of her child. If she chooses to keep the baby, it will mean making drastic changes in her life. She may have to give up the plans she made for her education and career.

In many cases, these difficult decisions are too much for the teenager to handle on her own. She may have intense feelings of fear, confusion, and depression. In that case, it is a good idea for the girl to get help by talking to a counselor at her school or a health clinic.

HAVING A BABY

"I felt really uncomfortable around everyone except my family because everybody really looked at me funny," said 16-year-old Jessica. "Towards the end, I was so big that even my boyfriend didn't want to be around me. I guess he was embarrassed."

Pregnancy can be an uncomfortable condition for a woman at any age. During the first few months the woman may have morning sickness, which means she feels sick to her stomach or throws up when she gets up in the morning. She is likely to feel tired and need more sleep. She may have sudden mood changes that she can't explain. During the last few months of the pregnancy she may have heartburn, backaches, swollen feet and hands, and leg cramps. Because her belly is growing so quickly, she may get permanent stretch marks on her skin.

Since her body is still growing, the teenage girl who becomes pregnant faces far greater health risks than an older woman. She is more likely to become anemic, which means her body does not absorb enough iron. This can make her feel weak and tired. It also makes it harder for her to fight infection. The pregnant teenager has a greater chance of developing toxemia. This condition, which occurs during the last months of pregnancy, is very dangerous for both the mother and the baby. Girls under the age of 15 are two-and-one-half times more likely to die as a result of their pregnancy than women aged 20 to 24.

Because her hip bones have not matured, the teenager may have more difficulty giving birth. She also has a higher chance of delivering her baby prematurely, or before the nine months needed for the infant to develop completely are over. Many problems that occur during pregnancy can be avoided if the mother takes good care of herself. She should eat a healthy diet, avoid alcohol, and not use cigarettes and other drugs. It is vitally important for her to get prenatal care (medical attention while pregnant).

Unfortunately, many teenagers do not follow these precautions, either because they are trying to convince themselves that they are not pregnant, or because they are hiding their pregnancy. Many girls do not get prenatal care until they are five or six months along, and a few only get medical care when they are ready to deliver the baby. This lack of care greatly increases the chances that there will be serious health problems for both the mother and her child.

CHANGES IN LIFE PLANS

Before she became pregnant at the age of 14, Nicole had big plans for her life. "First I was going to graduate from high school," she said. "Me and my cousin were going to travel the whole summer, just going to different places and seeing the world. Then we were going to come back and get an apartment together and both go to college. I was going to get my nursing degree. But I got in trouble first. Now I can't travel anymore."

Teenage girls like to imagine the kind of life they will have when they are adults. They may see themselves in exciting and interesting careers. They may picture the husbands they will marry, the children they will have, and the homes where they will live.

Once a young woman becomes a mother, however, everything changes. She can't make the same choices and doesn't have the same freedom anymore. As a mother, she is responsible for another person, someone who depends on her for everything: food, safety, and comfort. Everything becomes more complicated. "My life has changed a lot," said 19-year-old Melanie. "I can't just think always me, me, me. I have to take care of somebody else."

Karen found this to be true when she became a mother at the age of 18. "You've got to go to school," she said. "You've got to go to work. You don't know who's going to take care of your baby. You don't know if she's going to be sick and you can't go to work. If you don't go to work, you can't afford to buy her milk or food or diapers. Or maybe she needs a sweater because it's getting cold."

Other areas of a girl's life are likely to change when she becomes pregnant. Every year, about 40,000 teenage girls drop out of high school because they are pregnant. Many of them never go back. Teenage mothers are half as likely to graduate from high school as women who wait until their twenties to have their first child. They are also less likely to go to college.

If she doesn't complete her education, the teenager probably won't qualify for anything more than low-paying jobs. The average woman who becomes a mother before the age of 18 earns about half as much money as the woman who has children at an older age or has no child at all. Unless she gets help from her family or her child's father, it will be a struggle for the teen mother to support herself and her child. One out of every three teenage mothers turns to welfare to make ends meet.

Something as simple as dating becomes more complicated when a teenager is also a mother.

About one-third of the teenage girls who become mothers are married. Often the husband is a teenager himself, and the only reason they got married is because of the pregnancy.

A teenage girl who marries often gives birth to one or more additional children within a short period of time, putting more strain on a small family budget. Many young people cannot deal with so much stress. About six out of 10 teenage marriages end in divorce within six years. The young mother then finds herself with no high school diploma, no job skills, and two or three children that she must care for and support.

For teen mothers who are single, even dating or trying to date becomes more complicated. "I feel like I need a guy to count on," said Karen. "But I know it's going to be hard because what if he doesn't like my daughter? What if I get pregnant and have a baby with him? Is my daughter going to be put to the side and his baby put in front of her? This is what it's going to be like until I find a guy who is nice and takes care of me and my daughter...if there's a guy like that out there."

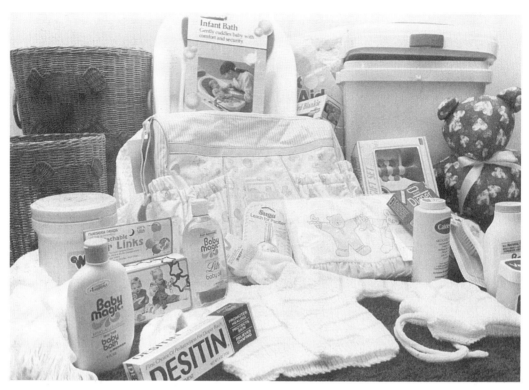

Just some of the paraphernalia that comes with motherhood: diapers; lotions, powders and salves for rash; feeding formula; medicines; bags to transport everything in . . . .

THE TEEN FATHER

When a teenage girl becomes pregnant, the father of the baby isn't always in the picture. In some cases, there is no real relationship between the boy and the girl, other than sex. In other cases, the relationship is over by the time the girl discovers she is pregnant. Some girls don't want the father to be involved. They don't believe that the boy would be a good partner or a responsible father. A few girls don't even tell the father about the baby.

In other cases, it is the boy who decides to take himself out of the picture. He may blame the girl for causing the pregnancy by not using birth control, or deny that the baby is his. He may simply refuse to take any responsibility for the child.

There are other reasons why the boy may keep his distance. His friends and even his parents might pressure him to avoid the burdens of marriage and parenthood. Perhaps the girl's parents blame him for the pregnancy and try to keep him out of the girl's life. Even the U.S. government welfare system's rules discourage the boy from being involved by limiting payments to a two-parent family with an unemployed father.

Nevertheless, many boys stay with their pregnant girlfriends. They try to be attentive fathers. They do their best to support the mothers, whether they marry them or not. This means the boys are required to make sacrifices.

Sixteen-year-old Paul dropped out of high school to work full time at a fast-food restaurant. Each week he gives $40 to $50 to his 16-year-old girlfriend to help pay for her prenatal care. "I knew it was going to cut out a lot of my privileges and fun on the weekend," he said. "I knew it was going to cost me. I wish I were older and that I had waited. The baby ain't even here, and already I have to pay."

Like Paul, many teenage boys drop out of high school and try to earn enough money to support a family. About four out of every 10 teen fathers earn a high school diploma by the age of 20, as compared to nearly nine out of 10 young men who wait until later to become parents. Unfortunately, it's very difficult for a young man with no high school diploma and no experience to make a good living.

Not all of the fathers are teenagers. Less than 20 percent of the babies born to teenage girls have fathers between the ages of 14 and 19. (The actual number of teen fathers is probably higher, because nearly 40 percent of teen mothers give no information about the father on their babies' birth certificates.) But unless the older man is well on his way to establishing a career, he may face some of the same difficulties as a teenager.

Dave, who is 23, was emotionally ready for parenthood when his 16-year-old girlfriend became pregnant. He and Rhonda live at his father's apartment, because they can't afford a place of their own.

"I wanted to settle down and meet someone and stay with them," he said. "I've been wanting to have a child for the last couple of years. I like the thought of being a father. We're getting married after she finishes high school. I want her to finish high school, and I want her to go to college, if that's what she wants, because she has to have her own life before we can start our life together.

"Eventually, I want to go back to school and learn sports medicine. I'd like to become a trainer at a high school, or something like that. Right now I'm working as a meat cutter at a restaurant. I don't make too much money, but it's enough to help out with the rent, buy groceries, and pay bills. There's not much left over for us, but that's the way life is."

Just as there are girls who intentionally become pregnant, there are boys who set out to become fathers. Generally, they are teenagers who are not doing well in school and live in impoverished communities where there are few jobs. Most of the families in their neighborhood survive on welfare. For them, having a child is the one thing they can point to as an achievement. Some of them brag about how many babies they have fathered.

Although these boys believe they are accomplishing something, they actually are making more difficulties for themselves and their girlfriends, not to mention the babies they are creating. There is a good chance their children will grow up with the same problems they had.

THE CHILDREN OF CHILDREN

Teenagers can become so involved with their own problems when facing an unwanted pregnancy, that they don't stop to consider how it will affect the baby. Being born to a teenage mother can result in serious and lasting consequences for a child.

Infants born to teenage mothers often have severe health problems. They may be premature, or may be born dangerously underweight (less than five and one-half pounds). They are more likely to die at an early age. They stand a better chance of having permanent disabilities such as cerebral palsy, mental retardation, deafness, and blindness. Some of the baby's health problems occur because the mother herself is still growing. However, many teen moms put their babies at further risk by not taking care of themselves and not seeing a doctor until late in their pregnancy. Teenagers who get prenatal care throughout their pregnancy have a much better chance of giving birth to a healthy baby.

For a teenage mother and her family, a baby's health problems can make a difficult situation even worse. Besides having to cope with the emotional stress of caring for a sick child, they will probably have to deal with enormous medical bills. For example, the average cost for treating a low-weight infant during its first year of life is $35,000. Medical care for a normal baby during the first year can be $2,000.

The problems do not end there. Children of teen mothers are more likely than other children their age to have low achievement scores in school and have to repeat a grade. They also have a greater chance of growing up in poverty. Many of them grow up to become teenage parents themselves.

The child of a teen mother also stands a better chance of having emotional problems than another child born of older parents. The child may grow up without a father and be raised by a mother who is so overwhelmed by her own problems, that she may be unable to provide the love and attention her child needs. Helping a child grow up properly is very hard when the parent is still immature.

Some teenagers simply can't cope with the responsibilities and difficulties of parenthood. They may feel frustrated and resentful about the freedom they have lost. Sadly, some take it out on their children by neglecting or abusing them.

"I get sad when I see my friends and their kids are all dirty," said Karen. "It's terrible. All my friends want to do is party. They leave their kids with a babysitter, or with people they don't even know. I don't think that's right."

Some babies born to teen mothers end up moving from one family to another. The teenager may have a difficult time deciding what to do. She doesn't seem able to care for the baby herself, but she can't make up her mind

AN EXTRA SEVEN POUNDS COULD KEEP YOU OFF THE FOOTBALL TEAM.

Become a father before you're ready and you may always wonder what else you could have been.

THE CHILDREN'S DEFENSE FUND

When adolescents have a baby, they inherit a whole new set of difficult responsibilities. Some of teenage parenting's demands will be difficult to cope with for both young fathers and mothers.

whether to give it up for adoption. She may leave the baby with her parents or other relatives, hoping to come back for the child at a later time. The girl may turn the child over to an agency that will place it with a foster family while she tries to resolve her problems. In some cases, the child is shifted from one home to another for years. It's not hard to understand how such a child would grow up feeling unwanted.

THE TEENAGER'S PARENTS

Needless to say, nothing will ever be the same for the pregnant girl's family once she decides to have her baby. The teenager's parents must deal with their own feelings of anger, guilt, and disappointment. "When I found out Marina was pregnant, all I could think of was that she let me down," said one mother. "Those years of teaching her moral values just flew out the window—it was like a slap in the face. I felt as if she did it to hurt me personally." Another mother, Ronnie Gunnerson, wrote about the feelings she had after she discovered her 16-year-old stepdaughter was going to have a baby:

"Are we supposed to accept the popular notion that we failed this child and that therefore we are to blame? Not when we spend endless hours and thousands of dollars in therapy trying to help a girl whose behavior has been rebellious since the age of 13. Not when we have heart-to-heart talks until the wee hours of the morning, which we learn are the butt of jokes between her and her friends. And not when we continually trust her only to think afterward that she's repeatedly lied to us about everything there is to lie about.

"Even as I proclaim my innocence in my stepdaughter's folly, I will carry to my grave, as I know my husband will, the nagging fear that we could have prevented it if only we'd been better parents."

Parents react to the pregnancy of a daughter in a variety of ways. Some become so angry that they throw the girl out of the house, forcing her to find somewhere else to live.

"My mom, she's the type that if she gets mad, she'll kick me out, no matter how late it is," said 18-year-old Karen. "I tell her, 'My daughter is my responsibility. Wherever I go, she'll go.' Just recently I got kicked out of my house for a stupid reason, just because I was talking to my ex-boyfriend on the phone. My mom said, `Karen, you have messed up all of our lives!' I thought I was doing real good because I go to school and I have a job on Saturdays. But I guess I wasn't, so she told me I had to leave. I'm looking for at least a little room to rent. Right now I don't have anywhere to go. I don't know what I'm going to do."

Other families pull together and find a way to help the teenager. Eighteen-year-old Yolanda lives at her mother's house with her boyfriend

Rudy and their five-month-old son, Angel. Yolanda's five younger brothers love to play with the baby and take him for walks in the stroller. Her five-year-old brother asked if he could take Angel to his kindergarten class.

Yolanda and her mother share household chores, and both take care of the younger children.

"If I need help, my mom helps me," Yolanda said. "She respects me more now. She doesn't tell me what to do with Angel. She explains and gives me her opinion. She doesn't get mad if I don't do it like she said to do it."

Sometimes it is the grandparents of the baby who end up raising the teenager's child. This is what happened to Hal and Janet, a couple in their late thirties, when their 16-year-old daughter Vicky had a baby.

"She wasn't an average teenager," Janet said. "She was in and out of juvenile hall. I think she felt like if she had a baby it would straighten her life out and solve all her problems. Then after she had him, it was just too much for her. She couldn't handle it."

"When she was pregnant, we talked to her about adoption," said Hal. "She didn't want to do that. She wanted to raise the baby. She wanted something to love her, something she could love unconditionally. She just didn't realize there was going to be so much responsibility."

"After the baby was born, at first I think she tried," said Janet. "Then I kept him every weekend or half the week, and his other grandma kept him the other half of the week. And then it got to where she just left him with anybody."

"She left him with a 10-year-old girl one time," Hal said. "Whenever we'd get him, he'd be filthy and hungry. She didn't know how to deal with him. We caught her screaming at him, every dirty word you could think of. He was terrified of her.

"She would drop him off over here and then she would come over and get in a fight with her mother. She'd say, 'I want my baby right now,' but she'd have nowhere to go. Janet would say, 'No, you're not taking the baby.' So Vicky would call the police. What could they do? They had to give him to the mother. The last time she did that it was three o'clock in the morning and the police came. They were just about ready to give him to her, but I said, 'Wait a second, check under his diapers. I think he's been beaten.' They checked, and they saw bruises, so they took him to a children's shelter. That's when she lost the baby, then and there.

"He has definitely enriched our lives, and we enjoy him a lot, but sometimes we get mad when we think about how he came into our life. We're locked up for 20 years now. Financially, we were just about to get our heads above water and maybe have a few things, but we're not going to now. There's definitely some resentment there. But, you know, he's such a sweet kid. What are you going to do? Put him in a foster home?"

ADMIN
FQHC
PC
PN
FPL
billing
Rent 700
Util 80
HH 15
Food 125
Car Ins. 125
CarMaint 40
CarSav 200
HIns 80
Pers. 25
Clothes 25
PC 20
1615
$13/hr
$2490
BBF 200
BBS 100
BBC 100
BBMP 75
BBHIns 100
$875

3

A COMPLICATED PROBLEM

"We see developing a population [of teenage mothers and their children] who have the cards stacked against them from the beginning. They are setting themselves up for failure, and it's costing society enormous amounts of money."
—Irene Goldenberg

W hy are so many of today's teenagers taking chances with their future by becoming sexually active? Why are so many of them giving up the last years of their childhood to jump into the responsibilities of parenthood?

There are no simple answers to these urgent questions. Teenage pregnancy is a complicated problem. The choices teenagers make about sex are affected by many different things in their lives. These include their relationships with their parents, the kind of friends they have, the way they feel about themselves, the kind of neighborhood they live in, how well they are doing in school, and their goals for the future. Many teenagers themselves don't seem to have a clear idea about why they are drifting into sexual activity.

Since teenagers are trying to become grown-ups, it's easy to see why they might have trouble deciding what to do about sex. Many adults are confused about it, too. Most adults still believe that the

Teens must sort through a maze of conflicting signals from friends, families and society about whether to become sexually active. Sex education can be one important way of coping with the problem of teenage pregnancy.

traditional family is the ideal, with mom, dad and the kids living together in one home. But often their own lifestyles don't reflect that image. Many teenagers have seen the adults around them divorce and then begin dating or living with other people. Adults tell teenagers not to have sex, to wait until they are married, but many don't follow their own rules.

Teenagers also get information about adults and sex through television and the movies. What they see on their favorite TV programs and in the theaters tells them that sex is easy, romantic, and exciting. There is little to warn teenagers about the possible consequences of sex, including unwanted pregnancy, AIDS, and other sexually transmitted diseases. There is even less information that tells teens how to be responsible about sex. The same TV networks that air sexy afternoon soap operas refuse to run commercials about contraceptives. Adults can't seem to decide whether sex is good or bad.

American attitudes about sex and marriage have gone through a lot of changes during the past four decades. Many of the rules that people followed during the 1950s were challenged and rejected during the 1960s. Today, many adults don't know whether they want to go back to the old rules or accept the new ones. They may not even be sure what the new rules are. Many parents have a tough time figuring out what to tell their teenagers about sex.

"I belong to a whole generation of people who grew up under traditional rules about sex," wrote newspaper columnist Ellen Goodman. "We heard all about the rights and wrongs, shoulds and shouldn'ts, do's and don'ts. As adults we have lived through a time when all these rules were questioned, when people were set `free' to discover their own sexuality and their own definition of morality. Now...we are the new generation of parents raising the next generation of adults. We are equally uncomfortable with notions that sex is evil and sex is groovy."

WHY TEENAGE PREGNANCY CAUSES PROBLEMS

There is nothing new about teenagers having babies. It has been an accepted practice for thousands of years. During earlier times, when most people had shorter lifespans and many infants and children died, teenage women were encouraged to marry young and start having children as soon as possible. Teenage marriage and motherhood are still common in many countries throughout the world.

In the United States, however, teenage pregnancy is a real problem because most of the girls who are becoming pregnant are not prepared—either financially or emotionally—to become parents. By having a child before they are ready to deal with such a large responsibility, these young females create serious problems for themselves, for their children, and for the society in which they live.

During the past two decades, the number of teenagers who became pregnant increased dramatically. In 1989, for example, 36 out of every 1,000 young women between the ages of 15 and 17 gave birth. This is more than double the birthrate for the same age group back in the year 1970.

Another troubling aspect is that pregnancy is occurring among girls of younger ages. It is becoming more common for girls as young as 12 to get pregnant. It is not hard to see how a pregnancy would be even tougher—both physically and emotionally—for a 12-year-old than an older teen. Approximately two-thirds of teenagers who are becoming pregnant today are unmarried. This is another big change from 1970, when less than one-third of the pregnant teens were single. This means that many of today's teenagers are becoming responsible for a child's life before they get the chance to establish a life of their own.

"I regret having the baby, in a way, because I wasn't ready," said 16-year-old Nicole. "I wanted my whole life planned. I wanted to finish college, have a stable job, get married, and have a nice home first. But things don't always work out that way." Having a baby can set off a chain reaction of problems for a teenager. She may find it too difficult to finish school with a child, so she drops out. Without a high school diploma or any work experience, it will be tough for her to get a job. If she does get a job, it probably won't pay much. It will be difficult to make ends meet and provide everything a growing child needs. Since only a few teenagers receive any support from the baby's father, she may end up depending on her family—if they can afford it and are willing to help her. Or she may have to collect welfare, which doesn't go very far. Unless she can find a way to complete her education or get job training, it will be very difficult for her to establish herself as an independent, self-supporting adult.

Another sad aspect of teenage pregnancy is that it tends to repeat itself from one generation to the next. Many of today's pregnant girls have mothers who were also teenagers when they became parents. A lot of those mothers are single or divorced, and undoubtedly many struggled to make a living. Because they were young and inexperienced, they may not have done a very good job of raising their daughters. It is not hard to understand, then, why their teenage daughters continued the cycle by looking elsewhere for affection and acceptance. Some thought they could find it by having sex. Instead of solving their problems, however, they created new ones when they became pregnant.

"I think families are like a chain," said Karen. "My mom had me when she was 18. I had my daughter when I was 17. Then I think, oh my God, I did it one year before my mom did, maybe my daughter is going to have a baby when she's 16.

"I'm not a good role model for my daughter. How am I going to explain to her why I did all this stuff? Why I had a baby too soon? She could say, `Mom, you did this at this age, why can't I?' What could I say? I do that to my mom. I tell her, `You had a kid when you were 18, so shut up.' So I guess I have to wait and see if my little girl turns out like me. I hope not."

A PROBLEM AMONG AFRICAN-AMERICANS

T eenage pregnancy is a particularly big problem among African-American communities in the United States. In 1988, there were 111 babies born for every 1,000 African-American teenage girls, as compared to 54 babies for every 1,000 white teenage girls. Nearly half of the African-American women in America become pregnant before they are 20.

Almost 90 percent of the African-American teenagers who are having babies are unmarried. Most of their children grow up in homes without fathers, in the poorest inner-city neighborhoods where there are few opportunities and little hope.

"When you look at the numbers, teenage pregnancies are of cosmic danger to the black community," said Eleanor Holmes Norton, a African-American law professor at Georgetown University. "Teenage pregnancy ranks near the very top of issues facing black people."

Teenage pregnancy often repeats generations; this family includes a grandmother, her 17-year-old daughter and her young granddaughter. African Americans in particular have a high rate of teenage pregnancy.

Why are so many single African-American teenagers having babies? There are people who believe it is because the young mothers then qualify for welfare payments, and can support themselves and their children without having to work.

If this were true, one would expect that states with the highest welfare payments would have the highest rates of unmarried pregnancies. Actually, the opposite is true. States with higher than average welfare benefits tend to have lower than average rates of children born outside marriage. The state of Mississippi, which has the lowest welfare payments in the country, has the second highest percentage of children born to single mothers.

Leon Dash, a reporter for the *Washington Post*, came to a different conclusion about African-American teenage pregnancy after living in one of the poorest sections of Washington, D.C., for 17 months. He wrote: "In time it became clear that for many girls in the poverty-stricken community of Washington Highlands, a baby is a tangible achievement in an otherwise dreary and empty future. It is one way of announcing: I am a woman. For many boys in Washington Highlands the birth of a baby represents an identical rite of passage. The boy is saying: I am a man."

Marian Wright Edelman, president of the Children's Defense Fund, agrees. "Too many of America's poor and minority youths who have no hopes for better futures become parents too young because they do not think that they have anything to lose," she says.

Although there is a higher percentage of teenage pregnancy among African-Americans than other groups in the United States, African-American teenagers represent only a fraction of the total problem. This is because only 12 percent of the population is African-American. The majority of teenagers who are giving birth are white. In 1988, for example, there were 152,508 babies born to African-American teenagers, and 319,544 babies born to white teenagers. The percentage of teen pregnancy among African-Americans has gone down for a number of years, while the percentage among whites—especially girls under the age of 15—has gone up.

One of the biggest causes of teenage pregnancy seems to be poverty, regardless of race. In largely white communities where many people are out of work, the number of teenage pregnancies has risen. Thus, African-Americans may have a higher percentage of pregnancies because they are more likely to live in poverty.

African-Americans and poor teenagers in general are not the only groups affected by teenage pregnancy. Teenagers who become pregnant represent all races in the United States. They live in small towns and big cities. Some come from families that are very poor, while others come from families that are wealthy. Some flunk out of school and others are honor students.

The one on the left will finish high school before the one on the right.

Adolescent pregnancy isn't just a problem in America, it's a crisis. To learn more about a social issue that concerns all of us, write: *Children's Defense Fund, 122 C Street, N.W., Washington, D.C. 20001.*

The Children's Defense Fund.

Because teen mothers generally have less education and lower incomes, they will be more likely to need public assistance in order to survive.

A PROBLEM FOR THE COUNTRY

Every year billions of state and federal dollars are spent to assist teenage mothers and their children. When a teenager can't afford to pay for her visits to the doctor while she is pregnant or after her baby is born, her bills may be paid by the government through a program called Medicaid. Another welfare program, Aid to Families with Dependent Children (AFDC), provides the mother with money for rent and other living expenses. A needy teen parent can also obtain food stamps, which help pay for groceries. It is estimated that about one-third of families started by teenagers depend on these and other types of welfare support.

More than one-half of the money the government spends on Medicaid, AFDC, and food stamps goes to families that were started by teenagers. The money to pay for these programs comes from all of the citizens in the United States who pay taxes. As the cost of supporting teen mothers and their families goes up, lawmakers must decide whether to pay the higher cost by increasing taxes or taking money out of other programs.

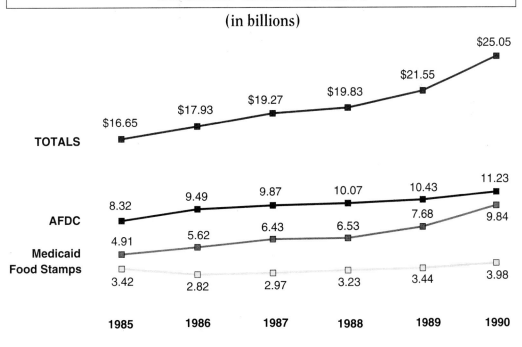

INCREASE IN PUBLIC COSTS DUE TO TEENAGE CHILDBEARING

(in billions)

Source: Center for Population Options

There are other ways that society pays for teenage pregnancy. For example, many school districts spend extra money to provide special schools for pregnant teenagers and teenagers with children. Then there are the costs for foster care, day care, and special education for these children.

Thousands of teenage mothers and fathers who drop out of school may never become productive citizens. That is a big loss to the country. The children they bring into the world will probably not get a very good start in life, and they may grow up to repeat the mistakes of their parents. It's not difficult to see why many people consider teenage pregnancy to be one of the major problems facing our country.

CHANGING TIMES

A re there more teenage pregnancies in the United States today than ever before? No. In recent history, the time when the highest proportion of American teenagers were having babies was during the 1950s. In 1957, 97 out of every 1,000 girls aged 15 to 19 gave birth, as compared to 54 out of 1,000 in 1988.

Of course, a lot of things were different 40 years ago. It was common for young women to marry soon after they graduated from high school, when fewer

INCREASE IN BIRTHS TO TEENAGERS IN THE UNITED STATES OUTSIDE OF MARRIAGE

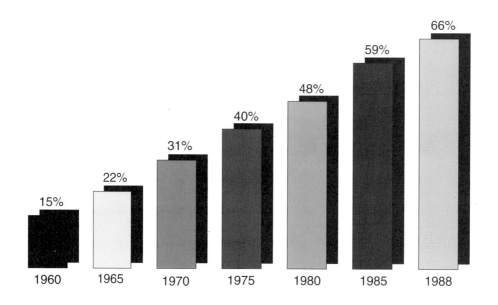

Source: National Research Council, Panel on Adolescent Pregnancy and Childbearing

women went to college. During the 1950s, nearly one-quarter of all 18- and 19-year-old women were married. Many of these teenagers who became pregnant wore wedding rings.

The 1950s were also a time of economic prosperity for a large percentage of Americans. It was fairly easy for a young man to start a career and earn a good living, even without a college degree. Many young families were able to afford their own homes and comfortable lives. Few mothers expected to work outside the home.

Attitudes about sex were different at that time, too. A girl was expected to earn her white wedding gown by remaining a virgin until after she was married. (Young, single men, on the other hand, were generally expected to gain some sexual experience before marriage.) An unmarried woman who became pregnant was considered a disgrace. If she kept the baby, she had little chance of being accepted as a decent member of her community. Her child was called "illegitimate" or a "bastard," and was treated like an outcast.

Many of the rules and attitudes about sex and marriage have changed since then. One reason has been the gradual change in the status of women that began when they fought for and won the right to vote at the beginning of the century. Another reason was development of new birth control methods, especially the pill, which was introduced in 1960. These new preventive measures made it easier for women to plan when or whether to have children, and to have sex without worrying about getting pregnant.

The 1960s were a time of turmoil and change. Many old ideas and rules were challenged. The feminist movement demanded equal rights for women in education, politics, and the workplace. More and more women attended college, started careers, and ran for elected office.

Young people also challenged some of the old rules about sex. Teenage girls had always been told that they must "save themselves for Mr. Right," while young men were allowed to "sow their wild oats." Since women now could use contraceptives to have sex without getting pregnant, some women believed they should have the same sexual freedom as men.

Then came the "sexual revolution" of the 1960s, when it became more acceptable for couples to live together and have children without getting married.

Television also played a major role in the changing of American attitudes. Some people say that television encouraged or even caused some of those changes, while others say it only reflected changes that were already happening in society. Either way, it's easy to trace changes in attitudes by watching the changes in television during the past four decades. During the 1950s, for example, even a married couple could not be shown together in one bed. Now there are very few sexually explicit situations that are not shown on TV.

Do other countries with cultures similar to that of the United States have the same problems with teenage pregnancy? The answer is no. In countries such

Peer counselors at a high school sex education class demonstrate the proper use of foam, one form of female contraception. Sex education is more common in Europe and Canada than in the United States, which has a higher rate of teenage pregnancy.

as Canada, the Netherlands, France, and Sweden, the percentages of teenagers who become pregnant are much lower than they are in the United States. This is true even though teenagers in those countries are just as sexually active as the teenagers here.

What appears to make the difference is the attitudes in these other countries regarding sex education and contraception for young people. Young people are given information about sex and pregnancy prevention—either in school or at family planning clinics. Teenagers are encouraged to use birth control and can easily obtain inexpensive contraceptives.

In Swedish schools, for example, children begin learning about sex when they are seven. By the time they are 12, they have been given information about various kinds of contraceptives. In Holland, television has played an important role in educating the public by broadcasting programs about sex and encouraging the use of contraceptives. "We've been told that no Dutch teenager would consider having sex without birth control," said an American visitor to Holland. "It would be like running a red light."

Many people believe that these attitudes are much healthier than attitudes in the United States. Faye Wattleton, former president of the Planned Parenthood Federation, said, "While European societies have chosen to recognize sexual development as a normal part of human development, we have chosen to repress it. At the same time, we behave as if we're not repressing it."

IS EVERYONE DOING IT?

S ex is everywhere. It's on television, in the movies, on the radio, in rock videos, on billboards, in magazines. Everyone thinks about it, talks about it, jokes about it, wonders about it. Sex must be pretty important. Statistics indicate that among unmarried teenagers aged 15 to 19, 50 percent of the girls and 60 percent of the boys have had sexual intercourse.

But is everyone doing it? The answer is no, even for teenagers. Statistics show that roughly one-half of all American teenagers are sexually active, meaning that the other half of them are not.

Besides, statistics can be misleading. A teenager who has had intercourse once or twice, and then decides not to do it again until he or she is older, may still be listed in a survey as sexually active. In addition, many teenagers who are sexually active do not have intercourse on a regular basis.

Even the way teens talk about sex with their friends can make it seem like there's more going on than there actually is. Boys, in particular, sometimes are so anxious to fit in with a particular group that they make up stories.

"Guys will lie about it," said 15-year-old Laura. "I know a lot of guys who are virgins, and they lie about it. They don't want anybody to know."

Rhonda agrees. "If you go out on a date and you won't do anything with the guy, a lot of times the guy will come back and say you did do something," she said.

Many teenagers are making a definite decision not to have sex until later in their lives.

"I know for myself and I am very confident in myself that I will not do anything until I find the right person," said Laura. "I'm very old-fashioned, and I'm a Christian. I believe you have to wait until you get married. And if anybody says I'm a virgin or makes fun of me, I just say, fine, go ahead."

"In my mind, if you're going to have sex, where can the relationship go after that?" asked 15-year-old Erica. "You should have a lot of trust in the person you're with. Sex is a big step. I want it to be more special. I want to do it more for the love part than the sex. What kind of a relationship is it if you just have sex?"

Carlos, who is 18, said he tried sex when he was 16. Now he has decided to wait.

"As a matter of fact," he said, "me and my friends are kind of abstinent because we know about the horrors that are out there, like AIDS and everything. I have some friends who are into one-night stands, but that is not my style. To me, personally, it's not worth it."

4

ABORTION

"I just went along with what he wanted and what was expected of me. If I had had the choice, I probably would have made the same decision. I'm really glad now that I didn't have his child. But it should have been my decision, or at least our decision."
—Allison, remembering an abortion she had at age 16

Linda was 16 years old and the mother of a one-year-old boy when she became pregnant again by her 18-year-old boyfriend. "I was having problems and the doctor told me it was very risky for me to have the baby," she said. "I decided to have an abortion. I told my boyfriend, and he was for it, but when we got there he wasn't for it any more. It was a two-day process, because I was already 17 weeks along. The second day when I had the surgery it was just terrible. Afterwards my boyfriend just wanted to cry. He spent the night with me because I was afraid. I was just scared of something, but I didn't know what. I felt guilty. That night I had a very bad dream. I just kept seeing the same room with the bright lights and the stirrups and the nurses. After that, every time we got in an argument he kept throwing it in my face. `You killed my baby.' Things like that.

"It was hard for me to decide on that. But I guess I had to do it. It was for the best."

Many teenagers who become pregnant decide to have an abortion. They end their pregnancy by going to a doctor who removes the contents of the uterus. During the first trimester (the first 12 weeks

The decision to have an abortion is certainly one of the most difficult any woman ever has to make. Some teenagers choose to terminate their pregnancy; others believe they shouldn't.

of a pregnancy), this is a fairly simple procedure that can be done in a doctor's office or a clinic. There is almost no risk to the girl. An abortion in the later stages of pregnancy involves procedures that are more complicated and may require a brief hospital stay.

Depending on where she lives, a teenager may find it very easy or very difficult to obtain an abortion. In some states, a girl can go to a local health clinic for an abortion without telling her parents. She may even receive financial help through Medicaid to pay for the operation.

In other states, it can be very difficult for a girl to find a clinic or hospital that performs abortions. A teenager may be required to get written permission from one of her parents before having the procedure performed. Some states require a girl to talk to a counselor first, then wait 24 hours before having the abortion. Many states will not allow Medicaid money to be used for an abortion, unless the girl's life is in danger from the pregnancy.

Out of every 10 pregnant teenagers, four decide to have an abortion. In 1987, 406,790 women under the age of 20 chose to end their pregnancy. That accounted for about one-fourth of all abortions performed in the United States during that year.

MAKING A DECISION

Teenagers give a variety of reasons for choosing to have an abortion. Some want to hide their pregnancy from their parents. Some say they aren't ready for the kind of changes a baby would bring to their lives. Others say they simply aren't old enough to be a parent, or they can't afford to have a baby.

Some teens have the decision made for them. "I was only 14 years old," said Maria. "I found out I was pregnant. My mom got very, very mad and started hitting me. One night my boyfriend and his mom came over to my house. They said that I was too young, and he was too young. He didn't have a job, and we wouldn't be able to support the baby. So my mom and his mom made an appointment to have an abortion without me knowing about it. One morning my mom told me, `You're not going to school. You're going to go with me and his mom.' I said, `Where are we going?' and she said, `Don't worry about it.'

"We showed up at this place. I was so scared. I didn't know why, I was just there. It's like a regular doctor's office, but once you go past those doors it's a whole different scene. You see tile everywhere, those metal stirrups, bright lights. They told me to take off my clothes, and they gave me a gown. They told me to lay down on a bed. I remember meeting the nurse and the doctor. Then

No amount of peer counseling or sex education can prepare a pregnant teen for the difficult decision of whether or not to have an abortion.

Pregnancy
Effectiveness
Abstinence
Chance
Withdrawl
OTC

they gave me the anesthetic and I was out. "Afterwards, I felt bad, but then I felt it was for the best because I wouldn't have been able to take care of the baby. I didn't want to remember any of it."

Some girls say they felt an enormous sense of relief after they had an abortion. Their problem was solved, and they could go on with their lives.

"I'm really glad I did it," said Allison, who had an abortion when she was 16. "It really would have messed up my life if I had had a baby then. Instead, I was able to finish high school and go on to college. I'm in graduate school now, and I'm going to become a social worker."

For others, the abortion brings with it a heavy burden of sorrow. They feel depressed and guilty, and they grieve for the baby they didn't have. Sometimes these feelings don't come out until years later.

"When I got pregnant, I was 15 years old," said Sandy. "My mom told me if I didn't have an abortion, she would kick me out. So I had an abortion. I couldn't believe I was doing this, because I had always said I never would do it. When I woke up afterwards I was crying. I still hurt inside because of what I did. I feel bad about it."

Another young woman tells her experience: "When I was 18 years old, I had an abortion at a clinic in Los Angeles. They put me in a hospital gown. Then they gave me a jar, like the size of a mayonnaise jar, and brought me into a really big room. There were chairs in a horseshoe all around the room and there were women sitting in all of the chairs. Each one of the women had a jar that she was either holding or had put at her feet. When we were brought into the room for the abortion, we would give the jars to the nurse, and then when they did the abortion, they would put what they got out in the jar. I remember thinking at the time that it was really cruel making us carry in the jars to carry out the babies with afterward.

"When the doctor got there, it was like an assembly line. Outside the operating room, there was a smaller room, and they put three women on stretchers in there. And in the hall they would have the next woman in line on her stretcher. They would do the abortion on the first woman, and then bring in the next one, and put a new one at the end of the line.

"When it was my turn, I was taken in. It was a big room, and it was cold and it seemed really dark. I was crying and the nurse told me not to cry, that it was not going to hurt. I remember thinking I wasn't crying because I was afraid it was going to hurt. I was crying because I didn't want to have that baby aborted. But my boyfriend wanted me to, so I did it.

"When I got home, I was cramping and I was depressed. I thought that even though my boyfriend said we would have other kids, that if he had loved me enough it wouldn't have mattered that it wasn't the right time. He would have said to go ahead and have that one."

ABORTION AND THE LAW

During the past ten years, abortion has become an extremely emotional issue in the United States. On one side of the issue are people who call themselves "pro-life." They believe that abortion is murder and therefore should be illegal. On the other side are those who describe themselves as "pro-choice." They believe that it should be up to the woman to decide whether or not she has an abortion.

Before 1973, abortion was illegal in most parts of the United States. A doctor who performed an abortion could be arrested and sent to prison. But there were still many women, including teenagers, who did not want to have a baby and who would do almost anything to end their pregnancy.

Women who had enough money could travel to a state where abortion was legal. There a doctor would perform the procedure in a hospital. Women who could not afford to go to a doctor sometimes tried to end their pregnancy by drinking large amounts of castor oil, by punching themselves in the stomach or throwing themselves down stairs, or by using metal coat hangers or other objects. Many women injured themselves terribly or became very sick with infections. As a result, some of them were never able to become pregnant again. Some of them died.

Other women sought out illegal abortionists. Some of these abortionists were doctors who could perform the operation correctly and safely. Others were people with little or no medical training. These abortions were often performed in dirty rooms with instruments that were not sterilized to prevent infection. Many women who went to illegal abortionists became very sick or died.

OUTCOMES OF TEENAGE PREGNANCY

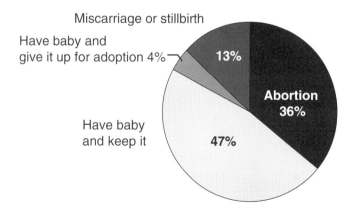

Miscarriage or stillbirth

Have baby and give it up for adoption 4%

13%

Abortion 36%

Have baby and keep it

47%

Source: National Research Council, Panel on Adolescent Pregnancy and Childbearing

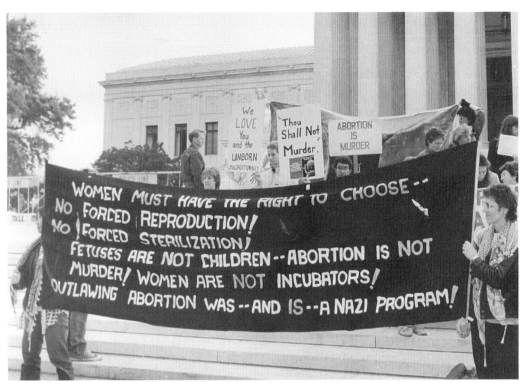

People who are pro-choice believe women should have the right to choose whether or not to have an abortion.

In 1973, the United States Supreme Court made a ruling in a case called Roe vs. Wade. The court declared that no state could make a law forbidding abortion during the first three months of pregnancy. The court did allow laws restricting abortion during the second trimester (third to sixth month) and forbidding it during the last three months, unless the abortion was needed to preserve the life or health of the mother. For a time it seemed that the matter was settled, and that women could have safe and legal abortions when they wanted them.

However, with each passing year the number of legal abortions increased. In the United States today, one in every four pregnancies ends in abortion. More than 1.5 million abortions are performed every year.

Many people are horrified by these statistics. They believe that women are using abortion as an easy form of birth control. They also believe that when it is easy to get an abortion, it encourages many people—including teenagers—to have sex outside of marriage.

The people who are pro-life have spent years trying to stop the practice of abortion. They have taken new cases to the Supreme Court, hoping the court would reverse its previous decision and allow laws that ban abortion. So far, the court has refused to do so.

However, the Supreme Court has allowed state laws that put restrictions on abortions. As of 1991, 20 states had laws that either required teenagers to have the written consent of a parent, or required doctors to notify the parents of a teenager before performing an abortion. Another 21 states had similar laws that were being challenged in the state courts. Supporters of these regulations say that a teenager is too young to make such a decision alone and that the parents have a right to know what their children are doing. "Parents generally have the best interests of their children at heart and will give them needed advice and support during a most stressful time," says Maura K. Quinlan, an attorney for Americans United for Life. Supporters also believe that these laws discourage teenagers from becoming pregnant. "If a young woman knows for certain that her parents will be notified of her pregnancy (not just that they might find out), she may be more likely to be more cautious about preventing pregnancy in the first place," Quinlan says.

ABORTION PROCEDURES

There are several methods of abortion. Which method is used depends on how far the pregnancy has progressed.

• **VACUUM ASPIRATION** - This method is used during the first 12 weeks of pregnancy. The entrance to the uterus is stretched open, and the contents are removed by an electric pump through a tube. The procedure takes about 10 minutes. There is very little risk to the woman. Most abortions (about 90 percent) are of this type.

• **D AND E (Dilation and Evacuation)** - This procedure is used during the second 12 weeks of pregnancy. This is similar to vacuum aspiration, but takes longer and may require additional instruments. Often the woman is under a general anesthetic. It can take from 10 to 30 minutes. About 10 percent of abortions are of this type. Clinics charge about $250 for an abortion during the first 12 weeks of pregnancy. Costs for abortions performed later can range from $350 to $1,000.

Those who oppose parent notification laws say that the majority of teenagers decide on their own to share their problems with their parents. The teens who decide not to may have very good reasons. One example would be a teenager with an abusive father who might beat his daughter if he found out she was pregnant. Opponents also argue that the laws cause pregnant teenagers to delay making a decision while they try to get the courage to tell their parents or try to find someplace where they can have an abortion without telling them. The delay can make it more risky and expensive to have an abortion if that is what the teen decides to do. If the teenager decides to have the baby, she may have missed several months of important health care.

Most of the states that require parental involvement in teen abortions have a "judicial bypass" system. This allows a teenager to obtain permission for

Some states place restrictions on the availability of abortions, especially to teenagers. Abortion is still highly controversial in the United States.

an abortion from a judge, rather than a parent. Opponents of the parent notification laws say this only creates more obstacles and delays for a pregnant teenager. It may be terrifying for her to present her arguments to a judge. Some teens avoid the entire process by traveling to a nearby state that doesn't have parental involvement laws and getting an abortion there.

OTHER OBSTACLES

P ro-life groups have used a number of other tactics to stop what they call "the national tragedy of abortion." Some of them demonstrate in picket lines outside clinics that perform abortions. They try to convince women not to go inside. Sometimes they try to physically block the entrances. Others resort to violence. Some clinics have been damaged or burned, and the doctors who work there have been threatened. In South Dakota, for example, there is only one doctor who performs abortions. His office in Sioux Falls is a cinder-block building with bullet-proof windows and burglar alarms. For 11 years he has walked through picket lines to get to his office. Another doctor in Pensacola, Florida, was shot and killed as he came to work. Many doctors have stopped providing abortions because they do not wish to deal with such problems or because of their own beliefs. Fewer and fewer new doctors are being trained to perform the procedure.

As a result of pressure from pro-life groups, more than 600 hospitals throughout the country have stopped offering abortions. There are also fewer clinics that provide the service. The ones that do have a tough time finding doctors who want the job.

What all this means is that even though abortion is still legal in the United States, it is becoming more and more difficult for many women—including teenagers—to obtain the procedure easily. Many people believe that it will become even more difficult in the future.

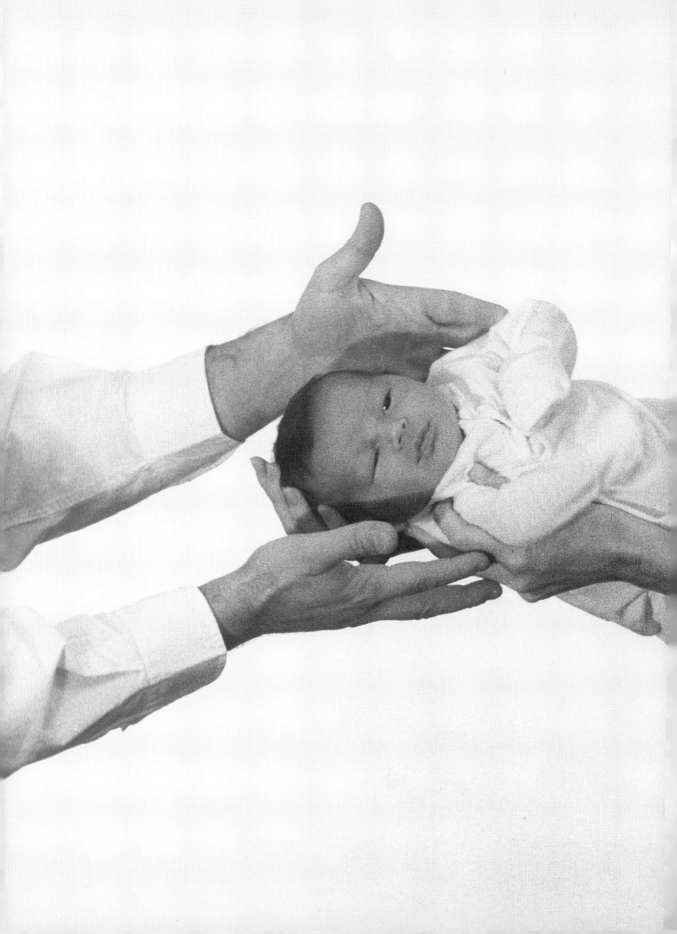

5

ADOPTION

"You'll never forget your child—you wouldn't want to. And there may always be some sadness. But knowing you've given your baby the best possible start in life, with the love and security of a good family, can make you feel better."
—Children's Home Society of California

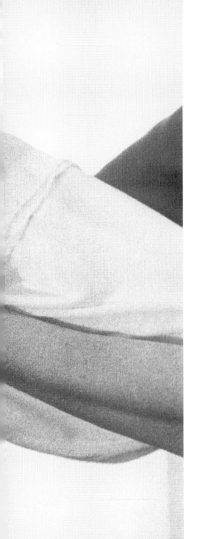

Lisa was 14 years old when she became pregnant. For several months she couldn't decide what to do. "I went back and forth in the beginning," she said. "At first I was going to get an abortion. I had my appointment, but when I went in there I couldn't do it. Then I thought I was going to keep the baby. I thought about that for about two months, and then my parents found out I was pregnant. My dad said, `If you keep that baby you can't stay in my house. I won't have anything to do with you. This will ruin your whole life.'

"My stepmom was really trying to help me. I think whatever I chose she would have been behind me. But my dad really wanted me to give the baby up, so my stepmom was trying to lean me in that direction. So we went to the agency to talk about adoption.

"Then when I was about seven months pregnant, I thought I wanted to keep my baby. I made all these arrangements to keep her. I was going to move to Oregon to live with my mother. She was all for it. My mom got pregnant when she was about 15, and she and my dad got married. So my mom thought if

Adoption is not the easiest solution to an unplanned pregnancy, but for many young women it is one they choose so that their baby can have a stable home life.

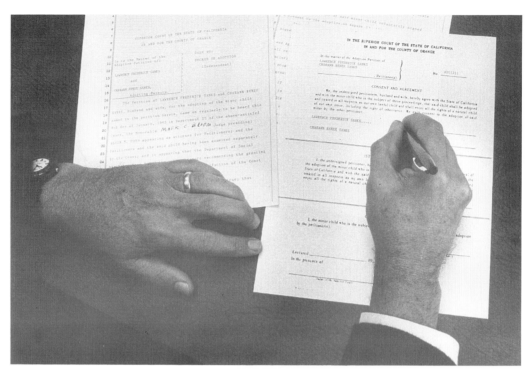

Attorneys can prepare a special legal document to make arrangements for a teenage mother who wishes to give her baby up for adoption.

you get pregnant, you have to get married, and you have to keep the baby and this is your whole life. Well, my mom and dad were divorced, and it became kind of a nightmare. I didn't want to go through that. My mom's an alcoholic, and she started calling me late at night to talk about moving in with her. I realized it wouldn't be really good to raise my baby in that kind of environment.

"My boyfriend was just awful. He was 18. When I told him I was pregnant, he just totally freaked out. He kept saying it was not his baby. So I didn't talk to him for about two months. He wasn't there for me at all. When I was about eight months pregnant I called him up, and we were talking about what I should do. He said I should give her up for adoption.

"So I went back to the adoption agency. My social worker there had this book that you look through with all these different people who want to adopt a baby. I was looking through it and then I saw Rick and Gloria. They stuck out. They looked really happy, really loving. They looked like they were really athletic, and I wanted my baby to be raised in that kind of environment. With my family, we just sat around the house. We didn't really go out and do things. I wanted something different for my baby."

A few weeks later, Ashley was born. Lisa spent two days with her in the hospital. When she left the hospital, Lisa went to the adoption agency to sign the relinquishment papers, which released the baby for adoption. Her daughter stayed at the hospital until her new parents picked her up later that day.

"When I left the hospital, it was awful," Lisa said. "My dad came to pick me up. I had to leave my baby in the room with the nurses. I was real upset. My dad had to pretty much carry me out of the hospital.

"For the situation I was in, I feel like I made the best decision I could. I think Rick and Gloria are doing a great job with her. I don't regret that I gave her up."

Like Lisa, some teenagers who become pregnant decide to give their baby to another family to raise. However, it is the option that is least chosen. Only about four out of every 100 pregnant teenagers release their baby for adoption. One reason may be that it has become more acceptable to be a single mother. Many girls are pressured by their friends—and sometimes their families—to keep the baby.

The girls who choose adoption believe that they are giving their babies a better life than they themselves could provide. "It was the right decision," said Sylvia, who gave up her baby when she was 17. "I feel good knowing that my baby is safe and that his new parents are taking good care of him."

ADOPTION PROCEDURES

Pregnancy outside of marriage is no longer considered as disgraceful as it once was. Adoption procedures have become much more humane. Most of the secrecy and shame has been taken out of the process. The feelings of the birth mother, and her need to know that her child is doing well, are taken into account. The child usually has access to information about his or her birth parents, which can be important for medical reasons. In many cases, the birth mother can stay in touch with the family that has adopted her child.

In most parts of the United States, teenagers who decide that adoption is the best solution can choose between two options. They can go through an agency or arrange for an independent adoption. However, every state has its own laws about adoption. Several states have laws forbidding independent adoption.

Agency Adoptions

About two-thirds of the adoptions in the United States are done through an agency. An agency is an organization that helps make the connection between a woman who would like to give up her baby and a couple that would like to adopt a child. Most agencies are nonprofit (meaning the money they take in is only used to run the agency). Many are associated with a particular religion.

Each agency has its own procedures and services. In addition to arranging adoptions and taking care of legal requirements, many of them offer other help, such as counseling for both birth parents and adoptive parents before and after the adoption. Some include shelters where the expectant mother can live until the baby is born. The agency may also arrange for a foster family to take care of the newborn child while the birth parents decide what to do.

Caseworkers at the agency spend a great deal of time talking to the birth mother and the birth father, if he is involved. They try to make sure that the teenager is very certain of the decision she is making. Many provide counseling, either individually or in groups, to help birth parents deal with their feelings of loss and grief. "Just as with a woman who has had a miscarriage, there's a tremendous sense of loss for women who surrender their babies," said Dr. William Pierce of the National Committee for Adoption. "Counseling is required to help these women get through it."

In the past, it was up to the agency alone to pick a family for the baby. Now many agencies permit the birth mother to make that decision. She can do this by looking through written information about each of the couples that have been approved by the agency. In some cases, she can meet the couple before making a decision.

Rick and Gloria, the couple who adopted Lisa's daughter, had tried for over a year to have a baby, with no success. They decided to adopt a child.

"We went through an agency because we wanted to be sure that the birth mother of the child we adopted had good counseling services and really had thought through her decision," said Gloria.

After going through an initial screening, Gloria and Rick were accepted for a home study by the agency. They were interviewed four times in their home. They also attended four training classes about adoption issues.

"During the interviews," Gloria said, "they asked us questions about the stability of our marriage, how we met, what we like about each other, what we fight about, how we resolve our problems, what our backgrounds are like, what it was like growing up with our families, ideas on discipline and raising children, what our values are. They were looking to see if we had any unresolved issues, any alcoholism or any other problems that would make it difficult for us to be parents. Plus, they sent us a 20-page questionnaire to fill out about everything.

"We had state and federal fingerprint checks and full medical checkups," she said. "We had to get references from friends and family and we had to get a CPR license and first aid training. I guess they figure if someone's entrusting their child to us, they want to know that we have some experience behind us.

"After we had our home study and we were approved, we put together two or three pages with pictures and information about us to put into this big notebook that they have at the agency for the birth mothers to look through. We also made a photograph album, so that if somebody was interested in us they could look at that and get more of an idea about the kind of people we are and the things we like to do. Then we just waited.

"We were only in the book about seven or eight weeks. The agency called and told us that a birth mother had selected us. I was really excited. I was in shock. I couldn't believe somebody had picked us."

"It was the happiest moment of my life," said Rick. "I was just ecstatic."

Open Adoption

After the baby has gone to live with the new family, the birth mother and adopting parents may decide to stay in touch with each other. This is called an "open adoption." In some cases, the birth mother and adopting parents do not exchange last names or addresses, but send letters and photographs to each other through the agency or through a friend. In other cases, there is no secrecy in the relationship. The birth mother stays in contact with the adopting family through letters and phone calls and may visit on occasion.

Lisa and the couple who adopted her baby chose to have an open adoption.

"We agreed to send letters and pictures of Ashley to Lisa every three months until Ashley was five, and then twice a year after that," said Gloria. "We had Lisa's address. Lisa didn't have our last name and would send letters to us through my girlfriend's address. Two years later, after we had adopted our second child, everything was becoming more open with adoptions. We were very comfortable with the birth mother of our second child and we had a real open relationship with her. So we approached Lisa about opening the adoption more. We wanted to know if she would be interested in having our phone number and talking on the phone

A BIG RESPONSIBILITY

For Gloria and Rick, adopting Ashley was a dream come true. They were finally able to have the family they always wanted. Two years later, they adopted a little boy. They have an open relationship with his birth family, too.

"Ashley is ours," said Gloria. "I couldn't love her any more if I'd given birth to her. She's our daughter."

"I feel like I love these kids even more than if they were our natural children," Rick said. "There's an extra burden of responsibility—not a negative one—an extra positive burden of responsibility because somebody has entrusted you to help them raise their child. You've got the birth family out there wanting you to do a good job, and you want to do a good job, too."

Gloria added, "I think we maybe cherish her a little bit more than a typical couple would because we had to go through so much to get her and because we have contact with the birth families. We are constantly reminded that their loss is our gain. And it makes us appreciate what it took to get her."

This attorney has handled thousands of adoptions, which he recalls fondly with the help of his photo wall, containing pictures of every couple who has adopted a child through him.

sometimes. She had moved out of state in the meanwhile. She was happy that we decided to do that. She came here during the summer and we saw her twice. It was the first time we had seen her in four years.

Lisa said the open relationship has made a difficult situation easier for her.

"If I wasn't in contact with my daughter, I would be hurting, and I would feel like I wasn't close to her at all," she said. "I think that would be bad. But even when I am in contact with them on the phone, it still hurts to hear her and feel like I'm not there for her. But I think I'd rather have it open. Going through all that pain is worth it because she knows who I am and knows that I'm kind of there. It gives me peace of mind to talk to her on the phone and to make sure that she's doing really good and that she's happy."

Independent Adoption

An independent or private adoption does not involve an agency. Usually the legal matters are handled by a lawyer. The birth mother may decide to choose this option if she already knows a friend or relative who wishes to adopt her baby. Another reason might be that the girl wants to be involved in choosing her child's family, but the agencies in her area do not handle open adoptions.

A birth mother who decides on independent adoption can find an adopting family in a number of ways. Sometimes her doctor, a religious leader, or a counselor knows of someone who would like to adopt a child. The girl may find a family through a newspaper advertisement, or she may go to a lawyer who specializes in adoption services. As with agency adoptions, the family that will receive the child sometimes pays expenses for the mother during her pregnancy and hospitalization.

There are a number of disadvantages in choosing independent adoption. One is that there is no counseling for the birth mother or adopting parents. This may make it more difficult for the mother to make a careful decision. The adopting parents, on the other hand, may not be fully prepared to accept a child and deal with the special issues and emotions involved in an adoption.

Problems may arise if there is only one lawyer representing both the birth mother and the adopting couple. Since the adopting couple is probably paying the fees, the lawyer may be more concerned about their needs and wishes rather than those of the birth mother. The birth mother may be pressured into a decision she is not ready to make. This can be avoided if both parties have their own lawyers.

Another disadvantage is that the adopting family is not checked out before the adoption. Usually the couple takes the baby home from the hospital and then files a petition with the state to adopt. The state sends out a social worker to study the adopting parents and decide whether they are fit to

A BOND OF TRUST

Louise and Ron tried for seven years to have children. Their doctors could not discover why Louise could not get pregnant. Finally, the couple turned to an adoption agency. They were introduced to Beth, a 19-year-old woman who had given birth to a boy but could not raise him. When the baby was five weeks old, the adoption was completed. Louise and Ron have stayed in close contact with Beth.

"I think most parents feel they have to be the best parents they can be," said Louise. "But I also felt the added pressure of raising Brian and taking care of him because someone had entrusted him to me. It wasn't anything that Beth laid on us. But she chose us. I really felt that she was entrusting her son to us to bring up in the best way that we could. I didn't want to disappoint her.

"Beth had asked for four visits a year. I remember thinking, how is this going to work? As we got to know her, it was just like a relationship you have with anyone. It takes a while, but you start to know a person and the relationship builds.

"Now, Ron and I feel like Beth is a younger sister. We really care a lot about her. She invited us to her graduation from nursing school a year ago. I don't think she'll ever leave Brian's life."

Many people have become happy parents of children born to unwed teenage mothers.

have the child. Often, this home study doesn't take place until several months after the family has taken the child. If problems are discovered and the baby is taken out of the home, it can be a traumatic situation for everyone involved. In most cases, however, the adoption is approved. People who are opposed to this system say the state's home study is usually not thorough enough.

Carly chose to arrange an independent adoption when she became pregnant at the age of 19.

"I was about in my sixth month when I decided that I probably should go ahead with adoption and let the baby go to a home where I knew he would be provided for and I knew he would have a mother and a father," she said.

"I was going to a pregnancy crisis center, and they hooked me up with an attorney who handled open adoptions. What the attorney did was to interview me to find out my hopes and expectations for my child. Then he looked through his files for people who matched my expectations, and I could interview them myself. After talking to several couples, I found one that I liked. I felt really good about them. They were an older couple, financially stable, and they held the same religious values I did. They were very sympathetic about what I was going through, and they weren't pushy.

"I didn't decide right away. I went through a lot of counseling at the crisis center, and after a couple of months, I felt that they met the criteria that I wanted for the child.

"The couple kept in touch with me during the rest of my pregnancy. When the baby was born, the husband couldn't be there because he was in the military. But his wife was there in the hospital waiting room. I got to hold my son a few times shortly after his birth. The couple took him home a day later. That was a very difficult moment for me."

Carly is married now and has two children. She stays in touch with the adoptive parents who are raising her son.

"I feel I did the best for him that I could," she said. "Basically, I provided for him in every way. I still get to have him in my life, but in a different way."

"I definitely think it's an alternative to abortion," said Lisa. "Some girls think, oh my gosh, I'm pregnant. This can't happen. I'm going to just get an abortion and that's it. But that's going to affect you through your whole life. You're always going to think, I could have had this baby. I definitely think that adoption is a better choice than abortion any day."

6

THE TEENAGE PARENT

*"How can you watch your children grow if you can't even
watch yourself grow?"*
—Sandy, 16-year-old mother of two

J essica is 16 years old and the mother of a five-
month-old girl. She tells her story:

"My family never paid attention to me. My
mom and dad never cared about me, so I was living
with my grandmother. She was an alcoholic. I was
15 when I met my boyfriend Ron. We just got along
really good. We really cared about each other. We
had these plans to stay together forever.

"My friends were saying, 'If you don't have
sex with him, he'll leave you.' I never should have
listened to them, because it wasn't true. He was
going to wait as long as I wanted to.

"I didn't use any birth control. I thought I
was going to be a lucky girl, or something. I got
pregnant about six months later. I had my period
through my pregnancy, so I figured I wasn't pregnant. I kind of felt I was, but I kept it to myself. One
day I took a pregnancy test with my friend and it
came out positive. She said it wasn't right and she
made me believe it wasn't right. Finally I went to a
clinic to get a test and it came out positive. I went to
the abortion place, and they told me I was five
months pregnant.

"I went home and told my mom I had to
have the baby. I was going to do an open adoption,
but my family was saying if I gave up my baby for
adoption they were going to disown me. They would
never talk to me again. So I decided to keep it, even
though I knew it was going to be a lot harder.

*Teenagers who aren't careful may wind up being parents before
they themselves have grown up.*

Juggling schoolwork and motherhood can be both stressful and rewarding, but it is never easy.

"I'm still together with my boyfriend, but I don't know if we'll be together that long because we have a lot of differences that didn't come out until after I had the baby. He's not the same. He's afraid I'm going to mess around and stuff. He doesn't realize how much I want my baby to grow up with both parents, because I didn't have mine, and I know how that feels. So no matter what, I told him, we have to work out our differences for the baby."

Every year, about 500,000 pregnant teenagers decide to give birth to their babies. Like Jessica, some simply wait too long to have an abortion. For others, abortion is not a choice they would consider. "I think that it's wrong," said Nicole. "If you think you are old enough to be having sex, then you should be able to face the consequences. You should deal with the problem and not just kill someone when it's not their fault."

Very few girls decide to release their baby for adoption. Like Jessica, they may be pressured by family or friends not to give up their "flesh and blood." Feeling an infant growing inside one's body is a powerful, emotional experience, and the teenager may find it too difficult to break the bond with the baby she has carried for nine months. "I don't think I could go on living knowing that part of me is out there that I'll never be able to see and never be able to tell it why I did it," said 16-year-old Rhonda.

Whatever their reasons, teenagers who decide to become mothers find their lives changed in drastic ways. Many are asked to leave their school, or they drop out on their own. Those who wish to continue their education must do so by studying at home or by attending a separate school intended for pregnant and mothering teens. Some girls can't go back to school because they live in a district that has no school for parenting teens and they don't have anyone who will babysit while they go to classes. Some girls go to work to help support their baby.

"A lot has changed," said Yolanda, the 18-year-old mother of a five-month-old boy. "I can't just get up and go now. If it's cold outside I have to put a jacket and a beanie and gloves on the baby. If I'm going to stay out long, I have to make the bottles, make the cereal, bring an extra change of clothes. You have to think about the baby before you do anything. If he's sick, I can't go. I have to stay home. Or if there's a movie I want to watch on TV and he's cranky, I can't watch it. I have to go rock him."

Eighteen-year-old Karen finds she has taken on new responsibilities since the birth of her daughter seven months ago.

"I have to work hard, three times as hard as if I were single, without a baby," she said. "Now I have to bring her to school, make sure she eats, get her bottle ready, sit down, start doing my work. If something is wrong with her I have to stop doing my work, get up and take care of her. And there they go, two hours. My chances of graduating are like ten percent out of a hundred."

For Karen, as for other teen mothers, every day revolves around her baby.

"I get up at six in the morning and I get a bottle ready, because I know that she's going to be waking up any minute. She's going to be crying and she's going to be fussing. By 6:30 I'm changing her diapers and changing her clothes. I have her play with some toys or something and I get myself ready for school. I come to school and try to work as best I can. Then I go back home. I've got to cook, clean the house, take care of my little girl, and try to do some homework if I can. Once you get home you can't do much schoolwork because your little girl needs attention. She wants you to sit there and play. Then I just wait for my dad to come home around six. We eat and I feed my little girl. Then I do whatever I have to do. I go back to sleep and start another day just like that. I never go out, never. I don't even know what `out' means."

MONEY WORRIES

Taking good care of an infant requires a lot of money. A baby needs formula, diapers, blankets, and clothing. A baby should be taken to the doctor for regular checkups. If a child is not healthy—a bigger risk with a teen mother—there can be high medical bills.

Unless she has a family that is willing to support her and her baby, a teenage mom must find other ways to pay her expenses. Some girls take on jobs, even if they are still in school. Because of their age and lack of education, however, it is difficult to find a job that pays very well. In some places it is difficult to find any job at all.

If she does find a job, a young mother will have to deal with the same problems that any working mother faces. She will have to find a babysitter. She will have to ask her boss for time off when her child is sick. When she finishes her working day, she will have to find the energy to be an attentive parent, do household chores, and perhaps finish high school.

Unless she can find a way to earn a college degree, a teenage mother is likely to be stuck in low-paying jobs for a long time. For many girls, it is difficult to find housing they can afford. Many young mothers end up moving from the home of one friend or relative to another.

Some young mothers turn to welfare for help. "I applied for welfare, but I wouldn't recommend it," said 17-year-old Ramona, who has a two-year-old son. "Just to go over there and apply for AFDC is a hassle. I don't know how people could stay on it so long. You have to spend five, six, seven hours sometimes just waiting for the clerk to call you."

A teenage mother may turn to the father of her child for help, but some young men decide they don't want to take on the financial burden of supporting a child. Even if they are willing to help, many of the fathers have little to offer. Most are either teenagers or in their early twenties, with little education or job experience. It is often difficult for the father to make enough money to assist the mother and their child.

"My baby's dad calls every once in a while to say hi," said 19-year-old Melanie. "But he doesn't come over because he has two other kids, too. He doesn't help support the baby. The district attorney is looking for him, but the dad says he's not going to work because he doesn't want to support the baby."

"My boyfriend says that he's going to leave now, so I guess I'm going to be on my own," Karen said. "It's not such a happy life. If you're on welfare, you have your limit. You get about $500 a month, and from that I've got to pay rent, I've got to buy clothes, I've got to feed my daughter. It's real hard, real hard. Now that he's going to leave, I guess I'm going to have to live off just that money."

Young males who become fathers before age 20 often do not finish high school, making it more difficult to find a good job.

YOUNG FAMILIES

Candy and Jack live in a sparsely furnished apartment. She is 20 and he is 21. They have two sons, ages three and two, and Candy is four months pregnant. Candy collects welfare and Jack is off work, due to a back injury. They plan to get married when they can afford a big family wedding.

Jack was 18 and Candy was 17 when she became pregnant the first time.

"Her whole family wanted to see me, and every one of them blew up at me—her mom, her sister, and her brother-in-law," said Jack. "They started bombarding me with questions. 'How are you going to live?' 'Where are you going to stay?' 'How are you going to do this and that for the kid?' 'Don't you want to go to college?'

"They offered her a car if she would have an abortion. Because she didn't get an abortion, they kicked her out. And then my brother didn't approve of it, so he kicked us out. I was working part-time at a gas station, so I had to quit school to get more hours. We lived in motels for four or five months."

"My family said if I walked out the door, 'Don't ever come back asking for anything,'" said Candy. "It was hard. I felt unwanted.

"I was only in tenth grade. My family didn't think that I would finish school. My counselor told me about schools for pregnant teenagers, and when we moved here, we were right around the corner from one. So I got to go to school and I graduated.

"I was nursing my baby, and my doctor told me there was no form of birth control for when you are breast-feeding. So I got pregnant again. I only breast-fed my second baby for a couple of months, then I went back on the pill. But I had so many side effects the doctor took me off of it. Now there's this new form of birth control that they put in your arm and it lasts for five years. I had an appointment to have that done. In between going off the pill and getting that done, I got pregnant again.

"Sometimes I have regrets," she said. "I always wanted to finish high school, go to proms, and I never got to do that. I tried going to college, but it was too hard. I had both of the boys to take care of. It was hard doing homework and stuff. So I had to drop out of college."

"I was working, doing construction plumbing," said Jack. "Carrying tubs on my back, putting them in tract houses. But I hurt my back, so I'm not working now.

"At the company they asked me how come I didn't complain about this earlier. I told them, when you got two kids and your girlfriend at home expecting some food on the table, you don't think about your pain, you think about them.

"Her mom thought that I would leave. I was like most teenagers back then. But there was a sense of growing up, of becoming somebody. I credit that to the continuation school I went to, because they really put something in your noggin. We did struggle and we are struggling. We're dealing with it, good or bad, right? We got in this together, and we'll get out of it together."

Like Candy and Jack, many young couples who decide to become parents struggle to make a life for themselves. Thirty or 40 years ago, it was fairly easy for young people to do this. But the American economy and the kinds of jobs that are available have changed since then. Now a high school graduate will qualify for only the lowest paying jobs. Most young people have to spend years getting a college degree and work experience before they can get a stable, well-paying career.

STARES AND FUNNY LOOKS

Compared to a few decades ago, it is much more common and accepted for a teenager to be an unmarried mother. But many girls still feel self-conscious about their situation.

"It's hard being a young mom," said 18-year-old Karen. "People give you looks. They stare at you. If they don't see a ring on your hand, then they feel sorry for you. They say, `Oh, you're so young.' Or some other people say, `Oh, she's such a slut. Look at what happened to her.' And then they think that we don't take care of our kids. I take very good care of my little girl. She's everything I've got right now. She's all I've got."

Young parents find it difficult to do this, since they have already taken on the financial burden of a child. Rather than staying in school and working toward a future career, many teenagers drop out and try to get work to pay for the responsibility they have in the present. In some cases, the young couple moves in with his or her parents.

"My boyfriend is living with me," said Yolanda. "He's working. He makes soda machines for restaurants. He brings home good money, $400 or $450 a week. We help my mom with the rent and the bills. We're going to get married in a couple of years. But first I want him to get me out of my mom's house. My mom says things will work out better when we have our own place. I want to see how that works out first, see how we get along. Because if he leaves me, what am I going to do? I can't pay the rent.

"I know I'm very lucky. A lot of the girls I know don't have the father with them anymore. He stayed with me. He supports me, he buys things for the baby and me. He's nice. He doesn't hit me, he doesn't do drugs."

Only about one out of every three pregnant girls marries the father of her baby. Sadly, these teenage marriages often fail. The pregnancy may have forced the teenagers into a decision that they really weren't ready to make. They may not even know each other very well. Besides learning how to live together and resolve their differences, the young couple must deal with the pressures of making ends meet and caring for a new baby. These are tough challenges—even for older couples. Many teenagers simply can't cope with these difficulties. Statistics show that separation and divorce are three times more likely to occur among teenagers than among couples who wait until they are in their twenties to have children. The majority of teenage brides are divorced within six years.

FAMILY CHANGES

Some parents react to their daughter's pregnancy by rejecting her. "I thought I could count on my mom when I got pregnant," said Karen. "I thought she would help me. I called her right after they told me I was pregnant. She said, `Well, your kid's going to be a bastard, don't ever bring him here.' I think I cried for about a week." Karen's mother eventually changed her mind and allowed Karen and her daughter to move back home.

Other parents welcome the new baby into the family, even though it means added expenses for the family. Some teenage girls end up living with other relatives or with the parents of their boyfriend. While this can be very helpful to the young mother, it can also lead to problems. Sometimes there are disagreements about whose baby it is. Yolanda ran into this problem when she moved in with the parents of her boyfriend, Rudy.

Being pregnant doesn't automatically mean a teenager can stop working. Often their families cannot make up for the added financial burden of a new baby.

"Rudy's mom was taking over the baby," said Yolanda. "She says things like, `I'll give him a bath,' and 'I'll feed him.' 'I'll take him to the doctor.' She bought his clothes and his diapers and his milk. And it's like if she's buying all that, then I have no right to tell her that she can't take him. So I just moved out, and Rudy moved in with me. We live with my mom now. If I need help, she'll help me. She's more understanding."

"It's my child, and I want to raise her," said Karen. "I love my mom and my stepdad giving her all that attention because it makes me feel real good. But they get to the point where they say, 'You can't feed her, I'll feed her.' Or, 'Don't change her, I'll change her.' They're trying to take over my daughter, and they're trying to raise her. I don't like that. She's my daughter, and I want to take full responsibility for her."

SWEETHEARTS AND FRIENDS

As they try to cope with their new life as a mother, many girls must also endure the heartbreak of losing a boyfriend. "I thought I was going to be fine and that me and the dad were going to stay together because he always said we were going to get married," said Ramona of her 19-year-old boyfriend. "Then he'd end up going to juvenile hall or something. When he'd get out, he'd say, `I'm going to get a job and things are going to be better between us.' It would be better for about a month, and then he'd be back with his friends. That's why we broke up. He said I demanded too much of him because I wanted him to call me so I'd know where he was. He said that was too much for him."

"Guys make promises, and then they leave," said Karen. "He'll say, `I'm going to do this and I'm going to do that,' and you think you've found your charming prince. And then he goes out. It's so easy for a guy to kick out. He just sees another girl walking down the street with a better body, better hair, better looking, and that's it. And then you're back where you started. But this time it's going to be hard, because you have a little girl in your arms."

Linda broke up with her boyfriend a few months before she gave birth to twin girls. "Sometimes I get so frustrated I just lock myself in my bedroom with them," she said. "I have the babies on the floor with a bunch of toys, and I just lay on the bed and cry. They look at me with a puzzled look. I'm even puzzled myself, because I don't know why I'm crying. I feel like a lonely space inside of me, I guess because I don't have their dad with me. But then I try to move on."

Some teenage mothers find that even their girlfriends abandon them. The active social life they once had comes to an end. "I lost all my friends," said Candy. "My best friend was okay while I was pregnant. After I quit my old school, she never talked to me. I see her every once in a while, but we really don't get to talk. None of my other friends have ever called. They pretend like they don't even know me. I guess it's because I can't go out and do things with them. It's like when they call, `Hey, can you go out with me tonight?' 'Well, no.' Click. Then they just don't call back. The teen moms at the other school I went to, they were going through the same thing I was. Some of them lost all their friends too. But we moms still talk to each other. We stick together."

"It's frustrating, because you're still young and all your friends don't even call you anymore," said Jessica. "They figure you can't do anything. So you sit there and think about them going out. My boyfriend played football. I could have played volleyball. I could have been really active and had fun. But I was just left with the baby. I told him, you're really lucky. You get to have fun still and I feel like I'm really tied down. He never really understood how I felt."

THE GOOD NEWS

When a teenager gives birth to a baby, it doesn't have to mean that she will never find happiness or success in her life. Some young mothers marry, have well-paying careers, and are good parents to their children. Some receive continued support from their family and friends.

One example is Veronica Velasquez, an 18-year-old high school senior in Ojai, California. Veronica, who was elected homecoming princess by her classmates, has a 23-year-old husband and a three-year-old daughter. She has a B+ average, works on the yearbook staff, and has won an academic award for her studies in French. On weekends she works as a cashier at a local hardware store. After graduating from high school, she plans to major in business at a local college.

Veronica said that she gets a lot of help from her husband and other family members. But she doesn't think that other teenagers should try to follow her example. "I hope people don't think it's an easy thing to do," she said.

Some teenagers say that having a baby has helped them change their lives in positive ways. "It helps me to have her," said 16-year-old Nicole. "Because now when I think of doing something wrong I think, no, you can't do that now. You have a little girl waiting for you."

Eighteen-year-old Karen said that having a baby helped turn her away from gangs and drugs. "When I see gang members, I still get attracted to it," she said. "I say, yeah, I used to be somebody. I used to be from a gang, and I feel like talking to them. And all I do is think of my little girl and then I say I'm not going to do that. So I can't get involved with gangs or drugs. I think if it wasn't for my daughter I would have been dead."

Some people assume that if a teenager becomes a mother, she will always be poor and on welfare, especially if she is African-American and lives in one of the poorest sections of a city. A team of sociologists from the University of Pennsylvania decided to find out if this is true. For 20 years they kept track of about 400 teen mothers in Baltimore, most of them African-American. They published their findings in 1990.

The researchers found that most of the teenage mothers went through long periods of hardship. Only one in three was married, and very few had married the father of their first child. In many ways they were not doing as well as women who had given birth to children when they were older.

Nevertheless, many of the women in the study eventually went back to school, took steady jobs, and got off welfare. Two-thirds of their daughters did not become parents as teenagers and most graduated from high school. A big reason for the success of these teenage mothers was the existence of special programs that helped them finish school.

Teenage parenthood doesn't have to be a dead end for a girl. It does, however, make many things more difficult. "I wouldn't wish getting pregnant on anybody, especially when you're a teenager," said Ramona. "It's too hard. I thought I was ready to have a baby, but now that I think about it, I'm not. I'm not emotionally or financially ready. Me and the baby's father aren't together, so it just makes it that much harder. I think you need to find somebody you're going to be with. You have to marry that person and get your life together first before you think about bringing kids into this world. When my baby is crying for his dad, I can't even tell him, here, I'll call him, because I don't even talk to him."

7

Responses to Teenage Pregnancy

"The best contraceptive is a real future."
—Children's Defense Fund

Teenage pregnancy is a major problem in America today, but finding solutions is just as complicated as the problem itself. Teenage pregnancy touches on a number of issues—such as sex education, abortion, and contraception—that are controversial and emotional for many people. This is one of the reasons why it is so difficult for people to agree on answers. In many cases, the ideas that some people have about the best way to solve a problem totally contradict those of other people.

Unlike many European countries, the United States does not have a nationwide program to deal with teenage pregnancy. Ideas about dealing with the problem tend to change as different Presidents come into office. In 1978, President Jimmy Carter's administration sponsored the Adolescent Health Services and Pregnancy Prevention and Care Act. This helped provide a variety of services for pregnant and parenting teens. Three years later, when President Ronald Reagan was in office, this program was eliminated. It was replaced by the Adolescent Family Life Act, which focused on abstinence programs that encourage teenagers not to have sex.

Although there is no national agenda for dealing with teenage pregnancy, there are hundreds of programs throughout the country that are focused on the problem. Some of these efforts are

Programs that help teenagers keep and raise their babies are mostly sponsored by private organizations and communities. There is no nationwide policy that assists teen mothers.

sponsored by state or local governments, some by school districts. Others are directed by churches, hospitals, Planned Parenthood and other health clinics, and organizations such as the Boys Club of America, the YWCA, the National PTA, and the Girls Scouts of America.

These organizations have responded to the issue of teenage pregnancy in two ways. The first is to assist teens who have already become parents, and the second is to encourage other teens not to become pregnant.

ASSISTING TEEN PARENTS

M any private and government organizations have looked for ways to assist young people who have become parents. There are numerous health clinics that provide free or low-cost medical services to pregnant teenagers, teenage mothers, and their children. Many organizations have opened homes for pregnant teens who need a place to stay. A number of programs are available to assist young parents in completing school, getting jobs, and establishing themselves as independent and productive citizens.

Many school districts have established separate schools for girls who are either pregnant or already mothers. These schools include nurseries where infants and toddlers can stay while their mothers go to class. In addition to regular academic subjects, many of these schools offer classes in nutrition, prenatal health, caring for an infant, and other topics valuable to a young mother. There are hundreds of schools like this throughout the country, and they have been very successful in helping teenagers finish high school.

Learning, Earning & Parenting is a state program in Ohio that encourages teenage mothers who are on welfare to go back to school. The program pays for transportation to and from school for the teens and provides child-care facilities for their children. Counselors advise the young mothers on how best to deal with the demands of going to school and raising children. Teenagers who attend school regularly get a $62 bonus in their monthly welfare check, while those who do not have $62 taken out.

New York state has an Adolescent Pregnancy Prevention and Services Program that is dedicated to lowering the incidence of teen pregnancy by working with at-risk males and females, pregnant and parenting teens, and their families.

Pregnant/Parenting Adolescent in Relationship is a new program begun by the Big Sisters Association of Boston. A teenager who is pregnant or has given birth is matched up with an older woman who spends at least four hours a week with her. The big sister gives the young mother friendship, advice, and encouragement. Other Big Sisters organizations throughout the country are starting similar programs.

At the Planned Parenthood Office in San Mateo, California, about a dozen teenage mothers meet once a week with a group leader. They talk about their children and learn about nutrition, contraception, child abuse, and other issues. At each meeting the girls are given $10 for staying in the program and not getting pregnant. Programs of this type were pioneered in Minnesota 17 years ago. They have been successful in reducing the numbers of children who are abused and neglected by teen moms. In addition, most of the teens who go through such programs finish high school, do not get pregnant again, and become self-supporting.

SEX EDUCATION AT HOME

One of the basic issues associated with teenage pregnancy is sex education. What do teenagers need to know about sex and when do they need to know it? Who should teach them? Does sex education cause or prevent teenage pregnancy? These questions have led to many heated debates.

Some people say that children should get information about sex from their parents, and only their parents. Others, like Sol Gordon, a professor at Syracuse University, tell parents it's impossible to keep young people in our society from picking up ideas about sex elsewhere. "You'll have to wrap your children in cotton and not allow them to leave their bedrooms, watch TV, or read newspapers or current magazines," he said. "You certainly can't allow them to have any friends."

Parents do play an important role in the education of their children. Studies show that teenagers who can talk to their parents about a lot of topics, including sex, are less likely to become sexually active at an early age.

Just as teenagers have many mistaken ideas about sex, adults have many mistaken ideas about teenagers. Some of these adult myths are:

"They learn everything they need to know in school."
"If they're not asking me any questions about sex, then they're not thinking about it."
"I know my son or daughter will come to me if he or she has a question or problem."
"If my teenager were getting in trouble, I would know about it."
"My kid doesn't want to listen to anything I have to say anyway."

Most teenagers say they would like to turn to their parents for information and guidance, but they don't feel comfortable doing so. The very thought of talking to mom or dad about a subject like sex makes them squirm. They don't like to admit to their parents that they are thinking about sex. Asking about a topic like birth control can be impossible.

Friends often tell each other things they won't tell their parents. Discussing sex and the need for sex education is harder between teens and their parents than teens and their friends.

Many parents are just as uncomfortable about discussing sex with their children. Doing so forces parents to admit that they themselves are sexual beings, and also makes them see their children as sexual beings. Parents are anxious to give their children the information they need to make good decisions, but they aren't sure they know enough to guide them properly.

"Me and my mom have open conversations about sex," said 16-year-old Yadira. "But when I talk to her about sex, she's giving me the one-sided thing. She says, 'You're my daughter, I don't want you doing this.' She tells me the bad things about sex. `Oh, it's painful the first time, and this and this could happen.' But she doesn't say it should be a special experience with someone you love, and the other good things. Parents need to give their kids both sides of the story."

"Parents need to lighten up, they need to get involved and talk about stuff," said Steve, who is 19. "Instead of threatening their kids and laying down the law, they should talk to them as people. That would be a lot easier on the kids than just saying, no, you can't do this. That's going to make kids rebel and want to go off and do it anyway."

SEX EDUCATION IN THE SCHOOLS

Some people believe that sex education in the schools is harmful. These people argue that teaching young people about sex, and especially teaching them about contraceptives, is like giving them the green light to become sexually active. They believe teenagers must be taught that sex should be reserved for marriage. "Teaching sex education in mixed classes to hot-blooded teenagers without benefit of moral values is like pouring gasoline on emotional fires," said Tim LeHaye, author of *Sex Education is for the Family*. "An explosion is inevitable."

Other people believe that ignorance is one of the causes of teenage pregnancy. They argue that teenagers who don't have enough information about sex and contraception are more likely to start having sex and initiating pregnancies. Since many parents don't teach their children about sex, the schools should. They also argue that teenagers are constantly under pressure from the media and their peers to have sex, and that many will succumb. It is better to give them the facts about contraception so that they don't end up with unwanted pregnancies.

Ask a roomful of teenagers about sex education, and there's no contest. Teenagers want information about sex. If they can't get it from their parents, they want to get it at school.

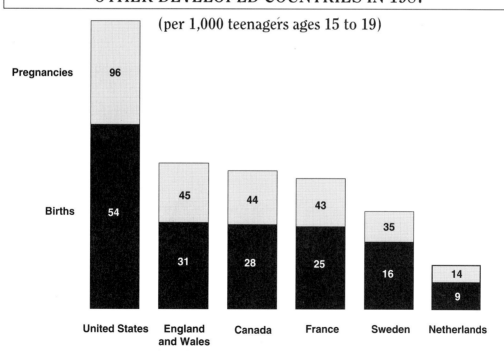

PREGNANCIES AND BIRTHS IN THE UNITED STATES AND OTHER DEVELOPED COUNTRIES IN 1987

(per 1,000 teenagers ages 15 to 19)

	United States	England and Wales	Canada	France	Sweden	Netherlands
Pregnancies	96	45	44	43	35	14
Births	54	31	28	25	16	9

Source: National Research Council, Panel on Adolescent Pregnancy and Childbearing

"Most parents are not open about sex and they can't talk to their kids about it," said 15-year-old Laurie. "Parents won't tell their kids what precautions they can take. They will just tell you, 'Absolutely, no way, you cannot have sex.' At school they give you more options, like 'If you were to have sex this is what you can use.'"

"The high school I was at wouldn't permit sex education, because that would be promoting sex," said 16-year-old Rhonda. "That's not right. They think that if they teach about it, then that gives you a reason to go out and do it, because then you think you know about it. But a lot of kids are going out and doing it because they don't know about it. They say, 'Oh, AIDS. You can't catch that.' I think if they helped kids and gave them sex education we wouldn't have as many pregnancies, and we wouldn't be finding as many babies in trash cans."

To improve the quality and availability of sex education, many Planned Parenthood clinics and other organizations are training young people to be peer counselors. These counselors learn about the aspects of sexuality, including birth control. They talk to teenagers one-on-one or in small groups at schools, community centers, beaches, county fairs, and other places where teens are likely to hang out.

Yadira, a 17-year-old peer counselor, argues that many school sex education programs offer too little, too late. "With a lot of the high schools that I know about, they only give a week or two of sex education in a health or science class in your sophomore year," she said. "That's a little bit too late, because by that time a lot of girls are already having sex, guys are having sex, girls are pregnant. And even if it wasn't too late, that's only two weeks of classes. For us, as peer counselors, it took us like a month or two to find out everything we needed to find out, and we still haven't found out everything."

Sonny, who is 16 and also a peer counselor, disagrees with the notion that teaching teenagers about sex will encourage them to try it. "I think it's the total opposite," he said. "I think a lot of times when there's a mystery about the whole thing, it's going to make you want to do it because you want to see what's going on. What's with this thing that everyone's so secretive about? And everybody's like, yeah, let's go try it. It enhances the wonderfulness of sex in their minds. When you teach kids about it, then it's no mystery."

Public opinion polls on the subject of sex education show that the majority of American adults are in favor of teaching young people the facts about sex, including contraception. About three out of four students take a sex education course before they graduate from high school. However, most of those courses are brief. Only 10 percent of students in the United States get 40 hours or more of sex education. Fewer than one-sixth of the nation's schools offer separate courses in sexuality.

In some states, the growing threat of AIDS is changing attitudes about sex education in the schools. Classes about preventing AIDS are now required in several states that previously opposed sex education.

SCHOOL HEALTH CLINICS

Another response to the problem of teenage pregnancy has been the establishment of health clinics on or near school campuses. These clinics provide a variety of free health services to high school and junior high school students, including counseling, sex education, pregnancy tests, and testing for sexually transmitted diseases. Some of the clinics also provide birth control pills or prescriptions for them. Some give out condoms.

By 1991, there were 327 such clinics throughout the United States. Most of them are operated by a local health clinic, hospital, public health department, or medical school.

The existence of these clinics raises almost as much furor as sex education classes. On the one side are supporters, who say the clinics are needed to help teach students, protect their health, and prevent pregnancy if they do decide to have sex. Teenagers are more likely to learn about and use contraception if they can get it where it is free, convenient, and confidential. The clinics do not encourage sexual activity, supporters say, because most of the teens who come to the clinic for birth control information are already sexually active.

Those who oppose the clinics charge that they take away the right of parents to be involved in the health decisions of their children. They accuse the clinics of encouraging teens to have sex and promoting abortion. Instead of teaching students to be responsible about sex, the opponents say, they merely help them escape the unfortunate consequences of their actions.

CONDOMS

In response to both teenage pregnancy and the spreading AIDS epidemic, various organizations have started handing out condoms in public places, including some high schools. Sometimes the schools themselves make condoms available to students. For example, at two high schools in Commerce City, Colorado, the school nurse and 15 teachers give condoms to students who ask for them. Teachers tell students that not having sex is the best way to avoid pregnancy and disease, but they also teach them about contraception. This includes demonstrations on the correct way to use a condom.

Condom distribution programs are extremely controversial. Up until a few years ago, the word "condom" wasn't even used in polite conversation.

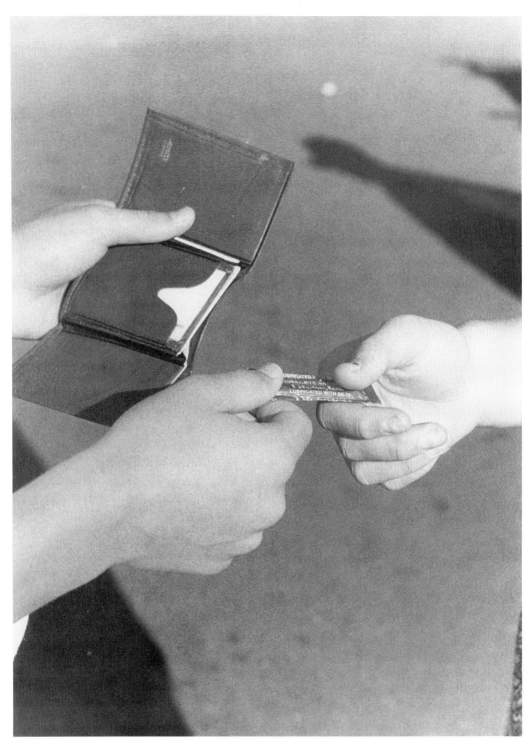

Condoms may help prevent disease and pregnancy, but abstinence is the only foolproof method. Nevertheless, more schools and cities are giving condoms away to young people.

Many people find it shocking that condoms would be passed out to young people. They believe that handing condoms to teenagers is another way of telling teens that they are expected to have sex.

. Many other people see condom distribution as a way of facing reality. They argue that some teenagers will have sex, no matter what anyone tells them, and the important thing is to protect their health. At the two Colorado high schools, with a combined attendance of 1,500 students, only 20 parents refused to allow their teenagers to participate in the program.

In other schools, information is not so readily available. "Last year there was this big thing where a gay group came to my high school and was passing out condoms," said 18-year-old Jeff. "I thought it was really special. I felt nice about the people involved because I thought they were showing us that they care about our generation, that they care about us as human beings, and that they want us to be safe, because they know we're having sex. I doubt that most people went out the next week and said, 'Hey, I got a condom now. How about I go experiment with sex?' If kids are going to experiment with sex, they're going to do it whether there were condoms passed out or not."

Lauren agreed. "I know a lot of people who aren't having sex, and it's not because they don't have a condom," she said. "Like me. I have really strong moral beliefs. Just because my boyfriend comes up to

---

EIGHT FACTS ABOUT SEX EDUCATION IN THE UNITED STATES

1. Twenty-three states require sex education to be taught in public schools. Another 23 states recommend it.

2. Sixty percent of girls and 52 percent of boys have taken sex education classes by the age of 19.

3. Eighty-nine percent of sex education courses include discussions of sexual abstinence.

4. Schools that offer sex education programs provide an average of about 42 hours of instruction in that subject. About five of those hours are devoted to discussion of birth control methods.

5. Eighty-eight percent of all sex education courses cover contraceptive methods, but only 52 percent provide information about where to obtain birth control.

6. Eighty-nine percent of instructors who teach sex education have received special training for that subject, but most say they need more help to effectively teach about preventing pregnancy and sexually transmitted diseases.

7. Several national surveys indicate that students who receive sex education are no more likely to be sexually active than their peers who have not had sex education. Sex education does not seem to be a major factor in a teenager's decision to become sexually active.

8. In one study, 22 percent of unmarried female teenagers who received sex education became pregnant, compared with 37 percent who did not have sex education.

The increase in early pregnancy is not the only reason why many people are concerned about teenagers and their involvement with sex. Another reason is the growing tragedy of AIDS, a disease that has already taken the lives of more than 120,000 Americans. Of the one million people who are infected with the HIV virus that causes AIDS, about one-fifth are in their twenties. Because the virus can remain hidden in the body for up to ten years after the person becomes infected, most of the HIV-infected people probably caught the virus during their teens. As of July 1990, 558 cases of AIDS among teenagers had been reported to the National Centers for Disease Control.

In addition, teenagers who have sex run the risk of contracting other sexually transmitted diseases (STDs) such as syphilis, herpes, genital warts, gonorrhea, and chlamydia. Every year, one out of every six sexually active teens contracts an STD. These diseases strike 12 million Americans a year, including three million teenagers.

The consequences of STDs can be devastating. Gonorrhea and chlamydia are the leading causes of infertility—the inability to become pregnant. Untreated syphilis can cause severe damage to the heart and brain. Genital warts have been linked to certain types of cancer. Many of these infections can be passed from mother to child at birth, resulting in blindness, brain damage, or even death for the baby.

Condoms provide some protection from STDs, but only if they are made of latex and used properly. However, they are not 100 percent effective in preventing the transmission of disease.

me and says, 'Oh, look. I got a condom,' I'm not going to say, 'Okay, we can do it now.'"

OTHER PROGRAMS

In California, the governor's office in 1991 launched a statewide effort called ENABL—Education Now and Babies Later. ENABL classes are presented to young people between the ages of 12 and 14 at schools and community centers throughout the state. The classes alert teens to the sexual pressures around them and teach them different ways to say no. The ENABL program also features television commercials and newspaper advertisements that carry the message, "If you're not ready, you're not alone."

Some programs focus on teenage boys. Since 1988, the National Urban League has launched more than one hundred projects aimed at teaching young African-American teens to be more responsible about sex. The message from the league is, "You don't have to be a father to be a brother." In New Orleans, the league has sponsored programs that encourage boys to stay in school. They provide job training and introduce teenagers to role models, such as African-American professionals and community leaders.

Another example of a program for boys is the Male's Place in Charlotte, North Carolina. This clinic provides free medical services and

A teenage boy must accept just as much responsibility as a girl in situations that might lead to pregnancy.

sex education programs for young men between the ages of 15 and 24. Outreach workers from the clinic provide medical screening and teenage sexuality workshops at prisons, Boys Clubs, church centers, and community schools. The clinic has also sponsored rap contests offering cash prizes to teenagers for the best raps on the subject of teenage pregnancy.

In New York, counselors from the Young Men's Clinic at Columbia Presbyterian Hospital videotape teenage boys playing basketball and break dancing on the street. They then invite the boys to the clinic to watch the tapes. The "commercials" are messages about sexual health from the counselors. Teens who come to the clinic also are offered condoms and information about preventing pregnancy.

Some organizations have come to the conclusion that sex education and birth control are only part of the solution. They believe that for many teenagers, becoming sexually active is just one part of a much bigger problem. These teens have low self-esteem and see no opportunities for themselves. They feel they have nothing to lose by becoming parents. This is particularly true for poor teens who are not doing well in school.

The answer, these organizations believe, is to give these teenagers hope for a future. "One thing we believe that keeps someone from getting pregnant, especially if you're poor, is if you have in your mind that you can be something," said Sharon Adams-Taylor, who works for the Children's Defense Fund.

The Door, a community center in New York City, is one place that works to give teenagers a future. Every year thousands of young people between the ages of 12 and 20 come to The Door for a variety of services. These include health care, counseling, sex education, and weekly discussion groups and workshops on a variety of topics. There are classes in arts, crafts, poetry, music, theater, dance, and gymnastics. Teenagers also can get assistance with school work, employment counseling, and job referrals.

These are just a few of the programs that have been set up throughout the country in response to the problem of teenage pregnancy. They have made a difference in the lives of thousands of young people.

SOME FINAL WORDS

Teenagers today are under a tremendous amount of pressure regarding sex. They may feel like they are being pushed and pulled from all directions. Some come to the conclusion that it is very important to start having sex. Others wish they hadn't.

"If I could do it again, I would finish school first," said Yolanda, an 18-year-old mother. "I would get to know the guy I was with...before I did anything like that."

"I wish I knew then what I know now," said Jeff, who became a father at 17. "I'd do a lot of things differently. I didn't think it would be this hard. I guess I thought it would never happen to me."

Many teenagers decide to have sex without thinking about all the possible consequences. Some of these teens don't know how easy it is to begin a pregnancy. Others, like Jeff, believe that "it can't happen to me."

For teenagers who have had to deal with an unplanned pregnancy, their view of early sex and its consequences changes dramatically. Their advice to other teens is simple:

> "Wait!"
> "Sex is not as important as everybody makes it out to be," said Rhonda, age 16. "It's not something you have to do. You should wait until you're ready and not let anyone push you into it."
> "If you think it's wrong, then it's wrong," said 19-year-old Melanie. "The only good friends are the ones who say, 'If she doesn't want to, or he doesn't want to, then it's fine.' That's a real friend."
> Sixteen-year-old Jessica agreed. "Maybe you truly feel close to someone," she said. "If that person really loves you, they will allow you to wait as long as you need to, until you are really ready."

It is important to remember that having sex can lead to very serious consequences, including pregnancy or AIDS. No matter what kind of pressures are being placed upon young people, however, it is up to each teenage girl and boy to make his or her own choice about sex.

ADDITIONAL RESOURCES

For more information about pregnancy and birth control, write to:

The Alan Guttmacher Institute, 111 5th Avenue, New York, NY 10003.

The Center for Population Options, 1025 Vermont Avenue, N.W., Suite 210, Washington, D.C. 20005.

Children's Defense Fund, 25 E. Street, N.W., Washington, D.C. 20001.

Planned Parenthood Federation of America, Inc., 810 7th Ave., New York, NY 10019 (800) 829-7732.

Sex Information and Education Council of the United States (SIECUS), 130 West 42nd Street, Suite 2500, New York, NY 10036.

For counseling about abortion alternatives:

A Call for Help (800) 537-2229.

FOR FURTHER READING

Bernardo, Neal, ed. *Teenage Sexuality* (Opposing Viewpoint Series). St. Paul, MN: Greenhaven Press, 1988.

Canape, Charlene. *Adoption: Parenthood Without Pregnancy.* New York, NY: Henry Holt and Company, 1986.

Charles Stewart Mott Foundation. *A State-By-State Look at Teenage Childbearing in the U.S.* Flint, MI: Charles Stewart Mott Foundation, 1991.

Dash, Leon. *When Children Want Children: The Urban Crisis of Teenage Childbearing.* New York, NY: William Morrow and Company, Inc., 1989.

Dryfoos, Joy G. *Putting Boys in the Picture: A Review of Programs to Promote Sexual Responsibility Among Young Males.* Santa Cruz, CA: Network Publications, 1988.

Edelman, Marian Wright. *Families in Peril: An Agenda for Social Change.* Cambridge, MA: Harvard University Press, 1987.

Elkind, David. *All Grown Up and No Place to Go.* Reading, MA: Addison-Wesley Publishing Company, 1984.

Guernsey, JoAnn Bren. *Teen Pregnancy.* Mankato, MN: Crestwood House, 1989.

Kolodny, Nancy J., Robert C. Kolodny and Thomas E. Bratter. *Smart Choices.* Boston, MA: Little, Brown and Company, 1986.

Lindsay, Jeanne Warren. *Pregnant Too Soon: Adoption is an Option.* Buena Park, CA: Morning Glory Press, 1988.

_____. *Teenage Marriage: Coping with Reality*. Buena Park, CA: Morning Glory Press, 1984.

_____. *Teens Parenting: The Challenge of Babies and Toddlers.* Buena Park, CA: Morning Glory Press, 1981.

McCuen, Gary E. *Children Having Children: Global Perspectives on Teenage Pregnancy.* Hudson, WI: Gary E. McCuen Publications, Inc., 1988.

McGuire, Paula. *It Won't Happen to Me: Teenagers Talk About Pregnancy.* New York, NY: Dell, 1983.

GLOSSARY

Abortion. A procedure performed by a doctor that ends a pregnancy by removing the contents of the uterus.

Abstinence. Avoiding sexual intercourse.

AIDS. Acquired Immune Deficiency Syndrome, a currently incurable disease that destroys the body's immune system, making it impossible for the body to fight off infections. The virus that causes AIDS can be passed on by sexual activity. As of now there is no cure for AIDS.

Anemia. A physical condition that may occur during pregnancy. The body does not absorb enough iron, leaving a person weak, tired, and less able to fight infection.

Birth Control. Methods of avoiding pregnancy. Birth control methods are called contraception.

Condom. A thin, flexible covering that fits over a man's penis. It is used during intercourse to help prevent pregnancy and diseases.

Contraception. The use of various methods to prevent pregnancy.

Ejaculation. The release of semen from the penis.

Genitals. The sexual organs of the body.

Intercourse. The sexual joining of a man and woman.

Medicaid. A federally funded program that helps those in poverty to afford medical care.

Menstruation. Monthly discharge of fluids from the uterus of a woman who is not pregnant.

Miscarriage. The end of a pregnancy due to the uterus ejecting the embryo or fetus before it is ready to be born.

Morning Sickness. A condition many women have during the first months of pregnancy. It causes a woman to feel nauseated or throw up when she gets up in the morning.

Ovaries. The two parts of a woman's sexual organs that produce eggs.

Ovulation. The release of an egg from a woman's ovaries.

Prenatal Care. Medical attention that a woman receives during the time she is pregnant.

Rhythm Method. Timing sexual intercourse for only the days in each month when a woman is supposedly less likely to become pregnant.

Semen. The fluid released by a man's penis during ejaculation that carries the sperm.

Sperm. The sex cells produced by a male that join with the egg produced by a female to create a baby.

STD. Sexually Transmitted Disease, a disease that is passed on through sexual activity.

Stillbirth. The birth of a baby that is dead.

Toxemia. A condition that may develop during the last months of pregnancy. Symptoms include high blood pressure, swelling of some body areas, and convulsions. If not treated, this condition is very dangerous for both mother and baby.

Uterus (womb). The organ inside a woman's body where a baby develops until it is ready to be born.

Withdrawal. A birth control method where the man removes his penis from a woman's vagina before ejaculating.

INDEX

A

B

C

C

D

E

F

G

W